How to Select and Use An Executive Search Firm

How to Select and Use An Executive Search Firm

A. Robert Taylor

McGraw-Hill Book Company

New York   St. Louis   San Francisco

London   Montreal   Paris   Sydney   Tokyo   Toronto

Bonnie Binkert and Michael Hennelly were the editors of this book. Al Cetta was the designer. Reiko Okamura supervised the production. It was set in Palatino by Achorn Graphics, Inc.

Printed and bound by R. R. Donnelley and Sons, Inc.

Library of Congress Cataloging in Publication Data

Taylor, A. Robert.
  How to select and use an executive search firm.

  Includes index.
  1. Executives—Recruiting. I. Title.
HF5500.2.T38 1983   658.4'07112   83-9920
ISBN 0-07-062959-5

  2 3 4 5 6 7 8 9 DOC/DOC 8 0 9 8 7 6 5 4

ISBN 0-07-062959-5

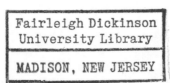

This book is dedicated to my colleagues in TASA and Arthur Young Executive Resource Consultants.

The mission of an executive search firm is to help its client organization to fill a key position by finding and placing the best executive for that position or by developing an alternative solution to the problem. Thus the selection of an executive search firm and the effective use of its services become just as important as the recruiting of an executive.

Contents

Acknowledgments

I wish to acknowledge the valuable assistance given to me in reviewing the manuscript by my partners, Juan Manuel Farias, Klaus Jacobs, Herman de Kesel, Paul C. Levison, William J. Messett, Edwin S. Mruk, Roberto Pelaez, R. Fred Rijke, Max Ruegger, Rubens C. Veras, and Kohtoku Watanabe.

Preface

There is a distinction between executive search consultants and "head hunters" or recruiters. Executive search is a profession. It is a specialized branch of management consulting. The truly professional executive search firms aim at helping client organizations to solve their executive vacancy problems in ways that are best for the client. They adhere strictly to professional rules and practices that are just as stringent as for other professions.

Good executives are in short supply everywhere and yet many of them could undertake much heavier responsibility. But they have no way of advertising or otherwise drawing attention to their talents while they are employed. A substantial number are not even aware of their potential. By bringing about better distribution and utilization of scarce executive talent, executive search firms perform an invaluable service to society.

There are countless examples of large and small organizations that have been given new life as a result of installing the right chief executive officer and, in many cases, an entire top team. With increasing frequency these beneficial changes are made possible by executive search firms.

One can understand, then, why these firms have grown and become more numerous. The use of executive search, which began in the United States, has now spread to all of the developed countries of the world and in some cases has permeated into the lesser developed areas where the recruitment of skilled managers is as important or perhaps even more important to the advancement of the economy.

The beginnings of executive search as a professional service to management took place more than forty years ago. By 1950, there were a handful of executive search firms. By 1960 the number had grown substantially. And by 1982, the number of firms providing executive search services was estimated at 646, with many if not most of the larger firms operating worldwide. Today the ten largest executive search firms have annual billings in excess of $10 million each.

Most of these largest firms achieved their preeminent position mainly for two reasons. Their clients recommended them to others. In addition, they were pioneers, moving into new geographic areas and developing new markets. Many equally good smaller firms chose to limit their growth and remain closer to home.

Specifically, the consulting services provided by most executive search firms are these:

1. The development of a clear definition of the problem. Why has it occurred? What solutions have been considered? Is recruitment from outside the company the wisest course of action? If so, is there complete agreement by all concerned on every aspect of the position and the executive who should fill it?

2. The preparation of a clear description of the company, the position to be filled, and the qualifications of the executive required. In many cases, counseling on the structure, content, organization relationships, and compensation is included.

3. Comprehensive researching of the industries and companies and geographic areas where candidates for the position might be found.

4. A thorough search with the objective of presenting the three or four best qualified candidates.

5. Penetrating verification of each candidate's record, qualifications, and reputation.

6. Assisting with the interviewing of candidates and selection of the most suitable.

7. Providing professional counsel on negotiations both to the hiring organization and to the candidate.

8. Helping the selected candidate to extricate himself gracefully from his present position, and to make a smooth move into his new position.

9. Following through to assist both organization and new executive with any problems that may develop during the executive's indoctrination period.

As can be seen by the scope of these services, it would be difficult for companies or other kinds of organizations to do the work successfully without a professional staff equivalent to that of an executive search firm. Some companies, particularly those that do extensive executive recruiting, do in fact take this approach, bringing the executive search function under their own roof, and using outside executive search consultants only for those recruiting assignments that are outside of their geographical areas or in very specialized fields. Many organizations find, however, that it is more practical or economical to use outside professional search consultants on an as-needed basis, rather than to staff up to perform the function internally. One of the big advantages of using outside consultants is the confidentiality factor: the company does not need to make its identity known during the recruiting process.

These are the reasons why an essential characteristic of a successfully completed executive search assignment is a close partnership relationship between client and search firm. The objective of this partnership is to bring about the best possible solution to the client's executive vacancy problem.

The purpose of this book is not to extoll the virtues of executive search firms, but to help managers to decide whether to use their services and, if so, how to obtain optimum results. The book provides practical common sense guides to help you to select the most appropriate search firm for your needs, to obtain optimum performance, and to avoid the costly mistakes that are being made every day in all of the aspects of executive search.

The underlying purpose of every manager is, after all, not to perform every function himself, but to accomplish the objectives of the organization through others. Businesses and non-business entities as well have become larger and more complex. As a result, the role of the professional manager has grown increasingly vital in keeping the economic structure of the world functioning. Even beyond that, it is the professional manager—particularly in his role of recruiter, organizer, and motivator—who helps keep human advancement moving forward in science, technology, education, government, medicine, social services and, in fact, all human endeavors. Without good managers to build strong organizations, what we see today as advancement in all human areas would be replaced by chaos.

In authoring this book, I bring to bear twenty-five years of experience as both a user and supplier of executive search services. I have seen or experienced many situations where companies have tried to find the best executive for a position by using techniques other than executive search, when they would have been better advised to turn to professional search consultants. I have also seen and experienced situations where organizations have used professional executive search consultants when they might have done the job as well or better by other means. And I have witnessed far too many situations where organizations have retained professional search consultants with high hopes, but by making a poor selection or by failing to establish a close partnership with the search firm, they have been sorely disappointed.

This book is intended to help organizations of all kinds to understand the circumstances under which an executive search firm should be retained, to select the most appropriate firm, and to achieve optimum results from the firm.

How to Select
and Use
An
Executive
Search Firm

There is always room at the top.

Daniel Webster

Chapter One

Problem: An Executive Position Must Be Filled

An executive search firm is a consultant to management. Like any professional service, it can be used with varying degrees of skill. The more skillfully it is used, the better the results will be.

An executive search firm is used by an organization seeking to strengthen its management by developing the best solution to its executive vacancy problems. A search firm cannot accomplish this purpose by itself. In fact, the best solutions occur when the organization and the search firm work smoothly together as partners. No matter how experienced, skilled, and professional a search firm may be in its approach, the success of an executive search project is nonetheless largely in the hands of the organization itself. This is an important point to remember in reading all of the chapters of this book. The point is made not to exonerate executive search firms from their responsibility, but to stress that an executive search firm's success can be only as good as its client organization permits it to be.

An executive search firm can help you to find the best solution to your executive vacancy problem. It can reduce and sometimes virtually eliminate the risks of making a wrong decision, but it cannot do this successfully alone.

As a specialized branch of management consulting, executive search firms have emerged as a necessary and respected part of the modern business scene for one reason only. Every organization that is dynamic, fledgling, growing, or large faces the continuing need to fill all of the existing and new executive jobs, and they cannot accomplish this essential, complex work effectively without turning, at times, to outside professionals. Companies and divisions that are starting from scratch would find it difficult or even impossible to succeed without executive search services. Executive search firms work primarily for business and financial organizations, but certainly not exclusively. It is becoming increasingly common for governments, educational institutions, foundations, charities, private clubs—in fact, organizations of all kinds—to turn to executive search firms when they have important management positions to be filled.

Sometimes a position must be filled simply because the organization is growing, and a new position has been created. In an even greater number of cases, however, the need is caused by change. Sometimes it is simply that an executive must be replaced because he or she retires, dies, quits, or is recruited away. Sometimes a key executive position becomes vacant because the incumbent is transferred or promoted to another, usually bigger position where he or she* is needed more.

Not uncommonly, an executive must be replaced because he is no longer able to perform satisfactorily, either because the job has outgrown him, he has lost his motivation or cutting edge, or his incompetence has been discovered.

Another, not uncommon reason for an executive change to be made is simply that the incumbent is unable to function smoothly as part of the management team because there is bad personal chemistry between the executive and his associates or boss, or because of unresolved and frequently unresolvable personality conflicts.

A large consumer products company had, on its own, brought in an unusually creative Marketing Director. They had assigned him to a division that was losing share of market. The division was headed by a good planner and organizer. The new Marketing Director developed a constant stream of new ideas that would have changed the plans and even the organization and the people in the division. The division head and

---

*Although it is recognized that executive positions are filled by both men and women, it would be cumbersome to use the two pronouns "he and she" when referring to executives throughout this book. Thus, the single pronoun "he" will be used to refer to both male and female executives.

the Marketing Director clashed to such a degree that the division's performance became even worse. A painful decision was made to replace the Marketing Director.

Often the problem of filling an executive position is thrust upon the organization, such as when a member of the management team quits or retires. At least as frequently, however, and usually more so, particularly in dynamic organizations, the need to make an executive change is—or should be—self-generated within the organization. In other words, the organization creates a problem for itself by recognizing the fact that it has a problem. For example, a company President recognizes that his company cannot continue to grow or capture the inviting profit opportunities that appear on the horizon unless a stronger Financial Vice President or Production Vice President is brought in to replace the executive who is in the job now. This is often one of the most difficult decisions for a President or equivalent to make because the incumbent in the position may be a close friend or someone who has contributed greatly to bringing the company to its present level of success. However, no Chief Executive Officer or Board of Directors worth their salt will sacrifice or compromise the interests of stockholders, employees, the rest of the management team, and all others with a vested interest in the company's success just to avoid the uncomfortable decision of making a needed executive replacement.

To say it succinctly, the management organization that is not continually renewing itself may lose its ability to compete and may eventually become increasingly characterized as dead wood.

This is not to say, however, that when an executive position must be filled the first step should be to dash out and sign up an executive search firm to solve the problem. You cannot simply turn the problem over to a search firm and expect them to solve it while you turn your back on the matter. Furthermore, it is wise to examine the alternatives before making a decision to bring in new executive blood from the outside.

For example, ask yourself the question, Does the position really need to be filled? Occasionally when an executive position is analyzed, it is found that the management structure can be strengthened or made more efficient by eliminating the position, combining it with another position, or redesigning it. Sometimes a job can be upgraded by adding additional responsibilities, or downgraded by shifting some of the responsibilities to another position.

In one company, the executive who was responsible for the smaller countries in Latin America resigned. The Head of Latin American Operations was on the point of recruiting a replacement when his Director of Finance reminded his boss that he had promised him an opportunity to manage a line operation. The financial executive was too high-powered to be assigned only to the modest responsibility for the small countries. The decision was made to add the line operation to his existing job and let him delegate some of his financial duties to his subordinates. The decision proved to be a sound one.

Assuming your analysis indicates that the position—in its present or redesigned form—must be filled, the next question to ask is, Can we fill it from inside the organization?

Again, before making the decision to replace an executive, all of the alternatives should be reviewed and examined. The executive who is presently in the position was obviously put there for reasons which, at the time at least, were or seemed positive and valid. What changes have taken place that have caused this executive to lose favor with his bosses? Are these conditions correctable? Your organization unquestionably has substantial investment in this executive. He undoubtedly has many pluses in addition to whatever negatives have caused the feeling that he should be replaced. Once you have clearly focused on the problem or problems that cause your dissatisfaction with him, give thought to whether these problems can be solved. Can the executive be salvaged through special training, through management development, through some effective form of remotivation, through counselling, through job restructuring, or perhaps by helping him to solve personal problems that have been interfering with his work performance?

A major conglomerate took this approach with an executive who was tagged for replacement, and discovered that through creative action the executive could be retained as a valuable member of the management team. In this particular case, the company was one that attached great importance to business planning and performance review meetings. An executive who had spent his entire career with the company and who had a brilliant technical record was promoted to Vice President, Engineering. Unfortunately, his performance in the big planning and review meetings was terrible. The President initiated steps to replace him. However, his fellow Vice Presidents went to considerable lengths to help him to overcome his stage fright and to prepare himself more thoroughly for the meetings. His performance in the meetings improved dramatically, and he was not replaced.

Assuming your analysis shows that an executive must be replaced, rather than an effort being made to salvage him, you still have one other big question to answer before activating an executive search outside of the company. Clearly, the question is, Can someone else in your organization fill this position? There are many advantages to filling an executive position from within, most of them obvious. The selected executive is a known quantity. And the other side of that coin is that your organization is known to him. He already knows your company's policies, people, customers, products, and idiosyncrasies.

Even beyond that, promotion from within can be made to have a strongly favorable motivational influence on people throughout your organization. Most organizations try to follow a program of promotion from within whenever possible for this very reason.

Finally, selecting your replacement executive from within your own organization reduces risk of failure and may avoid compensation problems and the increasingly high moving expenses and other costly, time-consuming, and disruptive new-executive problems.

For example, consider the situation that existed in one company where the decision had been made to go outside to replace a Vice President who had been promoted. After a lengthy consultation, the search firm advised the company that the existing compensation range and package would be unlikely to attract an executive who must measure up to their specifications. Nevertheless, the company instructed the firm to try. After six months of effort, it became clear that the search firm had been right. When the company weighed the problems and costs that could arise from a substantial upward adjustment of the compensation, they decided that it would be wiser to move a high-potential executive from a lower level in their own organization into the vacant position.

Let us assume that your company faces a situation where an important management position must be filled. No practical action can be taken to make the incumbent executive suitable for the position's future, and a suitable replacement for him is not available within your organization. The decision is made that you have to go outside. The following chapter deals with the various alternative approaches that are available to you.

Chapter Two

OK,
So We Have to Go
Outside

We have identified a problem in which an executive vacancy has occurred or is going to occur. We have concluded that it cannot be filled from within the organization. Therefore, we must bring an executive from outside the company.

Too often the first question that is raised is, How are we going to find the right man?

Long before that question is answered, much thought must be given to the nature, structure, content, authorities, and responsibilities of the position, rather than assuming that these are already understood. When this step has been taken, careful consideration should be given to the background, qualifications, characteristics, and personality—as well as the compensation—of the executive who should be brought in.

These important steps are thoroughly discussed in Chapter Six.

Many organizations make the mistake of assuming that essential key questions have already been answered. For example, Should the new executive immediately be given the full responsibility, or should his introduction into the entire position be arranged in steps?

A case in point was a major multinational that had never before recruited from the outside at senior levels. The management was encountering great difficulty with one of its important divisions. The company was losing share of market in a rapidly growing field in which it should have been a leader. The President came to the conclusion that neither the current head of the division nor anyone else in the company had the relationships in and knowledge of the marketplace needed to compete successfully. Reluctantly, they decided to go outside.

The company had long and strongly established characteristics. All of the executives at division-head level and immediately below had been with the organization for at least fifteen years. The company was planning to recruit an executive directly into the top position. However, when they consulted a search firm, it was pointed out that it would be impossible for an outside executive to step into such a position and hope to function effectively. Therefore, a plan was developed whereby the new executive would begin as the assistant division head and remain in that position long enough to understand the company and its people.

The search was successfully completed. It took eighteen months before the new executive could be moved into the division-head position. During the eighteen months he made valuable contributions, but his full potential for developing the market could not be realized until he headed the division, after which he more than met the tough goals that the company had set for the division. The wisdom of raising the question about his original introduction into the company was certainly proven.

Let us assume that you have decided to go outside and have answered a number of preliminary basic questions. At this point, you are ready to consider the question, How shall we recruit the executive from outside the company? You have four alternatives. You can do it yourself or engage an employment agency or hire a contingent executive recruitment firm or retain an executive search firm.

Your first question may be, Should we do it ourselves? Some companies have established their own internal recruiting organization to work on assignments at middle and senior management levels. Companies that have and expect to continue to have to recruit relatively heavily from outside are, in a number of cases, convinced that they can reduce costs and the time required by establishing their own internal executive recruitment organization. In such cases, they only turn to executive search firms when there is an overload or when they need an executive with experience in other parts of the world that they are not equipped to handle.

The advantages of this internal service are that it is usually less costly if the volume of recruitment is high enough. The internal recruiting staff is thoroughly familiar with the company and its executives. The vast amount of information that is developed as a result of searching can be maintained by the company in usable form for future recruitment decisions.

There are, of course, some disadvantages. Like the internal auditor versus the external auditor, there can be less objectivity and independence on the part of the internal staff. In addition, if the recruitment load fluctuates, the staff may be underemployed at times. Of greater importance is the matter of confidentiality. There are often situations like the case of "the burned-out executive."

In this case, a senior executive in the health care industry had been in the same position for almost ten years. For eight years the performance of his division had been superior and continued to be good. But more recently there were signs of deterioration. Important symptoms of the malaise were becoming apparent, such as the loss of some good executives, and poor morale. There were also increasing indications of a weakening position in the marketplace.

These symptoms caused much thought and effort to be given to helping the division head to improve. However, it became increasingly apparent that he had lost his drive. For various reasons, there was no other suitable opportunity in the company to which he could be moved. Finally came the painful decision that he would have to be terminated. There was no suitable replacement within the company. It was realized that it would take many months to find and bring in a replacement. In the meantime, the company was approaching the business planning season. In addition, the executive who was to be terminated was engaged in a delicate worldwide licensing negotiation in which his personal relationships were an important factor.

The company decided that a search would have to be conducted in strictest confidence. The burned-out executive must not be given any indication of the plans to replace him until the new man had been hired. At the right time, a fair and even generous termination arrangement would be made.

Under circumstances like these, it would be very difficult for an internal recruiting staff to handle the assignment. An executive search firm can conduct a search under these conditions without giving any clue as to the identity of their client. This element of strict confidentiality greatly increases the difficulty of conducting a search because many executives who are approached initially insist upon knowing the identity of the organization that has the vacancy. Nevertheless, strict confidentiality is one of the important ground rules of a professional executive search firm.

In addition to internal considerations, there are often external reasons for confidentiality. Does it matter if the business community or your competitors know that you are searching for a key executive to fill a specific senior position? Are you prepared to handle the numerous job applicants who will surface when job-hunting executives become aware of the search? Will you have problems if some of these applicants are customers or friends?

Another potential disadvantage of utilizing an internal recruiting staff may be the difficulty that some of them encounter in acting as true consultants to their managements. As previously indicated, objectivity and independence are difficult for an employee to maintain. It is often necessary for the search firm consultant who is handling an assignment to disagree with his client. It is true that he does not want to lose the client and that he will probably temper his disagreement accordingly. Nevertheless, if he is a true professional, he stands a better chance of emerging from such disagreements unscathed than does a company employee whose career with the company may be at stake.

Another factor is the breadth and depth of search experience and of research data that a good search firm possesses. There are some excellent internal recruiting staffs that can match the services of most search firms, but these are not too common.

Companies that have good recruiting staffs often find that they are best utilized for middle-management recruitment. The infrequent senior search assignments are handled by executive search firms.

For those companies that do not have a professional executive recruiting staff, a decision to try to recruit on their own is usually not a good one. Apart from the confidentiality problem, it must be kept in mind that an executive search assignment generally requires about 150 professional man-hours. There are few companies whose busy executives can afford to spend this much time on the recruitment of one executive, and because they are often not executive search experts, the probability is that far more than 150 man-hours of their time would be needed.

The customary practices of companies trying to recruit on their own, without a professional staff, consist of making inquiries among contacts within the industry, talking to law firms, public accounting firms, and to bankers. These efforts usually produce numerous well-meant recommendations on candidates who are seeking a change and are wide of the mark. Too often such activity results in bringing in a man who has a likable personality but who is far from the best solution to the problem.

Having taken into consideration the choice between doing it yourself and seeking an outside service to help to fill the position, the decision may be to go outside. There are three basic choices. Before considering specific firms, decisions have to be made on whether to use an employment agency or a contingency recruiting firm or an executive search firm. In making these decisions, it would be wise to apply the same criteria as the company uses in selecting law firms and public accounting firms. It might even be helpful to compare the decision-making process to that of selecting a restaurant, although in this latter case, there is certainly a major difference in the end objective of finding a good meal versus solving a complex executive problem. Nevertheless, we might compare an employment agency to a fast food restaurant, a contingent recruiting firm to a cafeteria, and an executive search firm to a good restaurant.

The employment agency obtains its prospective candidates through advertising and through résumés sent to the agency by people who are looking for a job. The agency provides its company clients with a substantial number of résumés, among which might be a qualified candidate. An employment agency tends to be a paper mill with little or no use of comprehensive interviews. The agency earns income from the job seeker or the company or both only when they place someone. The agency's motivation is to place as many people as possible as quickly as possible. The agency must, of course, achieve a certain degree of success or it could not remain in business, but it is highly unlikely that the best executive for the position will surface through the agency's advertisements and collection of résumés. Keep in mind that an employment agency can only present to you those people who are currently looking for a job.

The employment agency has its place, but not in filling upper-level vacancies. A good agency provides valuable services in helping to recruit people for clerical, skilled labor, lower-level professional, and supervisory positions.

Another possible choice would be a contingency executive recruitment firm, i.e., a firm that charges for its services only if it places a candidate with a company. Some of these firms function similarly to an employment agency but usually do not charge candidates for their services. They tend to work at somewhat higher levels than do employment agencies. Contingency executive recruiting firms usually interview their candidates. They do not charge retainers.

There are some contingency firms that aim at providing services similar to those of an executive search firm. Their problem, when they try to do this, is that they cannot afford to risk the average 150 professional man-hours needed to provide the full range of executive search services. It is difficult for them to function as a true consultant whose aim is to help the client find the best possible solution to his problem. This is because, like employment agencies, their entire earnings are dependent upon placing as many people as quickly as possible with companies. They can only bill companies for their services when an executive has been placed.

Contingent executive recruitment firms are often utilized for lower- and middle-level management positions. Also for those companies that are satisfied with simply finding an executive who meets the specifications and are not particularly interested in achieving the optimum solution to their problem, a contingent firm could be the right answer. The company does not have to pay any retainer but simply pays the contingency firm if an executive whom it recommends is hired.

Having weighed the pros and cons of the three alternatives of utilizing your own people to recruit for the vacant position or using an employment agency or engaging a contingent executive recruitment firm, there is still the fourth choice—an executive search firm.

The disadvantage of this choice is that you risk payment of retainers from the outset of the assignment without any guarantee that your executive vacancy problem will be solved successfully. But is this not also the case when you retain a top professional in any other field such as law, public accounting, taxes, medicine, or other areas of management consulting? In fact, professional executive search firms are management consultants who specialize in solving executive vacancy problems. The difference is that the results of the search firm's performance are more readily measurable than those of other management consultants.

But the question may still remain, Why should you choose to pay retainers to a search firm when you can obtain the services of an employment agency or a contingent executive recruiting firm without any financial obligation unless they supply you with an executive who can fill your vacancy? The facts about executive search firms, set forth in Chapter Three, will help you to answer this question to your own satisfaction.

Chapter Three

Some Facts About Executive Search Firms

If you have not already had extensive experience in retaining executive search firms, this chapter will help you to make the decision on whether to retain one for your particular executive vacancy problem. Brief answers are provided to questions most often asked about executive search. The subsequent chapters in this book cover these answers more thoroughly.

A. Why has the executive search profession grown so extensively?

There are several reasons. Probably the predominant one is the maturing of management as a professional function. This development brought about a realization that the success of an organization depends largely on the quality and performance of its managers. The organization with the best executives is most likely to move ahead of its competitors. Therefore, ways had to be found to develop the best from within and recruit the best from outside.

A second reason is the gradual understanding that executive search firms are the main means of bringing about better utilization of scarce executive talent. There is no way that a frustrated executive can advertise his desire for a bigger job that does not exist for him in his present organization. Nor can companies and other organizations usually broadcast their confidential executive requirements. Search firms became the much needed instruments for bringing underutilized executives into organizations in which their talents could be more effectively applied.

Another reason is confidentiality. The organization may not want the decision to be known either internally or within the business community. Under those circumstances a third party must do the searching, protecting the identity of the organization.

A fourth reason for the growth of the executive search profession is that the costliness of errors in executive selection became increasingly evident. The wrong man may hinder or even cripple the organization for years. The time required to indoctrinate an executive into a new position, give him sufficient time to demonstrate his effectiveness, the agonizing, time-consuming decision to replace him, and the costly internal or external recruiting process all over again have taught some hard lessons. Such events led to the recognition of the need for professional assistance in finding the right man for the position.

A fifth reason is that experience with executive search in turn brought about a better understanding of the special skills needed to find and bring into the organization the right executive for the vacant position. Among these are the definition of the true needs of the organization and the kind of executive most likely to fulfill them; a realistic appraisal of the difficulty in finding the right man and what it will cost to attract him; the ability to thoroughly search out the very best candidates regardless of where they may be or how invisible they are; the infrastructure and experience required to evaluate more than a hundred prospective candidates and select the two or three who would be the best performers; counseling the organization on handling candidates from the first telephone contact through the interviews and all of the other steps until the executive is in place; the especially useful role of a professional third party in negotiations between organization and candidate that are often difficult and complex; the special abilities needed to conduct confidential and delicate inquiries into the candidate's record, qualifications, and reputation in a way that will not create embarrassment for anyone yet leave no stone unturned; the ability to counsel the selected candidate in extricating himself smoothly from his present organization and community and in establishing himself in his new position; the ability to smooth out any problems for either the organization or the new executive during the beginning phase of their new relationship.

A sixth reason is the realization of the importance of an objective, independent, unbiased third party role in helping management to make critical executive staffing decisions. There is growing acceptance of the fact that organizations are often too strongly influenced by their own personal preferences, prejudices, habits, and preconceptions.

A seventh reason is that in conjunction with the growing professionalism of the management function, the need for more profound candidate specifications became evident. This development, in turn, made it necessary to search more broadly and deeply to find the best executive to meet these specifications.

B. How did the executive search function develop from the beginning to the present?

Prior to the existence of executive search firms, executive recruitment was conducted informally through personal contacts including bankers, lawyers, public accounting firms, management consulting firms, and the old boy network. Then came the provision, by some management consulting and public accounting firms, of executive recruitment services in the United States. The next development was the establishment, usually by people who already had some experience with these organizations, of small executive search firms. Some of these early firms grew into multi-office operations.

The multinational clients of search firms in the United States began to ask for professional services in staffing their overseas operations. At first, there were attempts to provide these services from the U.S., but it soon became evident that only by having qualified executive search consultants in overseas locations, could the same service standards be maintained.

When the first executive search service actively began in Europe, European companies and executives were certain that only American companies and candidates would be involved. Their opinion was that European culture systems would not accept the idea of executives being systematically moved from one company to another. However, as U.S. search firms became more active in Europe, they began moving European and British executives into U.S. multinationals to replace American expatriates and to meet their growing requirements. European and British companies soon realized that they too could not achieve their growth and diversification objectives nor be competitive without the help of executive search firms. As demand for these services increased, European and British search firms also evolved.

In Latin America, in the Asia Pacific regions and later, in South Africa, the history of executive search has been similar to the developments in Europe and the United Kingdom. At first, it was the U.S. multinationals that demanded services in these areas, especially as they sought to replace American expatriates with local national or third-country national executives. South of the U.S. border, Mexico was the first country in which international executive search services began. Subsequently, Brazil, Argentina, Venezuela, and Colombia became bases for international executive search offices. The sequence in Asia Pacific was Hong Kong, Australia, Japan, and Singapore.

Local companies in all of these areas were at first slow to utilize executive search services. They doubted that a foreign firm could help them with their local staffing, and they were unaccustomed to paying for such services which, in their eyes, had usually been provided free of charge by their banks, law offices, friends, and acquaintances.

Today, with the exception of Japan, the continuing substantial growth rate of executive search services outside the U.S.A. is occurring because they are being increasingly utilized by national firms.

Consultants with growing search firms everywhere left, in some cases, to start their own operations. Today, there are a few large firms with billings in excess of $10 million dollars per year, several medium-sized and scores of small firms. The large firms have their own practices outside the United States. The medium-sized firms have mostly made agreements with foreign search firms. Some foreign search firms have offices in the U.S.

C. Efforts to strengthen professionalism

During the later 1950s, leaders in the executive search profession in the United States decided that the time had arrived to establish a professional association. There were two basic reasons. State legislatures began to move in the direction of applying the same regulations to executive search firms as they had already done to employment agencies which, of course, offer an entirely different service. This would have imposed conditions that would have made it impossible for executive search firms to continue to function, such as government access to confidential files and regulation of service charges.

The other basic reason for the emergence of a professional association was that the necessity to set up standards became apparent if executive search was to gain recognition as an established profession. Accordingly, the Association of Executive Recruiting Consultants was organized. The name has since been changed to the Association of Executive Search Consultants (AESC). Today it is a well-known professional organization. The AESC has developed and published a code of ethics and professional practice guidelines (see Chapter Four). Firms that are members must adhere to the code and practices. Firms that apply for membership must prove that their policies and practices are in accordance with the standards required by AESC.

There are now over 60 member firms. Recently, the AESC Board decided to consider applications for membership from search firms whose operations are entirely or mostly outside the United States.

There are some search firms that have decided against membership in AESC but that maintain at least the same professional standards as do AESC members.

D. How are search firms organized and how do they function?

Search firms are usually mainly owned and controlled by their founders, until the founder either retires or dies and the often difficult transition is made to ownership and control by the next generation. The few firms that are broadly held usually did not start out that way. Some users of executive search believe that broadly held firms may be more inclined to function as a team.

Another important factor in the organization of search firms is the method of compensation of the consultants. In some firms, the consultant's compensation is determined entirely or largely by the amount of billings that he individually earns for the firm through bringing in clients and assignments and through working on assignments. This system motivates individual consultants. It sometimes leads to overloading and lack of teamwork.

The other method of compensating consultants is judgmental. They are paid salaries and allocated bonuses based on the judgments of their peers and superiors with regard to their contribution to the overall firm's performance. This system, in theory, reduces the tendency to overload and increases the likelihood of good team work. However, in either case, the performance of the firm is heavily influenced by the quality of the consultants and the effectiveness of management.

Some firms staff themselves with bright young executives, usually with graduate business degrees. Others prefer more mature, proven, senior-level executives. Between these two extremes are firms in which the younger executives are supervised and encouraged to develop by the more senior members of the firm, similar to the practices of major accounting and law firms.

Some firms use their "heavy hitters" to sell their services and monitor the work, leaving the search work to less experienced associates. In other firms, the man who brings in the work often handles the resulting assignment. There are, of course, many combinations of these practices, and this is particularly true when searches have to be conducted outside the country in which the assignment is taken.

There are large firms that have specialists for specific industries and functions. There are small firms that specialize. There are generalist firms that have demonstrated their ability to handle all functions and all industries.

E. How do executive search firms charge for their services?

Executive search firms usually base their service charges on the annual compensation applicable to the position to be filled. There are numerous executive recruiters who offer their services on a contingent basis, i.e., the client pays only if an executive is placed. However, the firms that are considered to be the most professional charge retainers from the outset of their work for their clients. These retainers are credited against the final basic service charge or a total charge based upon time expended on the assignment. The basic service charges usually range from 30% to $33\frac{1}{3}\%$ of the annual compensation. Some firms charge 35% or more for international assignments requiring searching in more than one country. Such expenses as long-distance phone charges, meals with sources and prospective candidates, and travel to interview candidates and meet with clients are added to the billings.

There are a variety of practices in charging the retainers. Some firms charge ⅓ of the estimated basic charge at the outset of the work, another ⅓ part way through the assignment, and the final ⅓ when the assignment is successfully completed. Others charge ⅕ of the estimated basic charge at the outset plus ⅕ per month. Most firms do not continue charging retainers if the work goes beyond the estimated time frame unless the delays are due to major changes in specifications or inability of the client to meet interview schedules.

Some firms, instead of expressing the basic charge in terms of percentage of the annual compensation, will quote a fixed amount based upon their estimate of the difficulty and the amount of work that will be required. Usually these fixed basic charges approximate the percentages charged by those firms that apply the 30% or 33⅓% or 35% system.

Multi-country searches are the most difficult to manage and are the most costly to search firms. Although many firms claim that they will conduct a thorough search in several countries for an international assignment, the truth is that they cannot afford to do this for a normal basic charge. Unless the client is willing to pay for extensive searching on a multi-country basis, the search firm is forced to compromise in order to avoid heavy losses on the assignment.

How is a search conducted?

The effective conduct of an executive search involves a number of fundamental steps. The first one, of course, is a thorough understanding and agreement between client and search firm of the organization, the position, and the specifications for the executive required to fill it. This information should be spelled out in writing.

The next step is research, conducted by the search firm's research department or by the consultant or both. The purpose of the research is to develop as much information as is needed on prospective candidates and sources of information throughout related companies, industries, functions, and geographic areas to enable the consultant to conduct such a thorough search that he can be confident that he is presenting to his client the two or three best candidates who can be found.

Based upon the research data, the consultant contacts scores of sources and prospective candidates, screens many of the prospects by telephone, and interviews those who are both interested and appear promising. The consultant should be in close contact with the client throughout the course of his search. Jointly with his client, they decide upon those two or three candidates who should be interviewed by the client.

The next step is presenting the candidates to the client, sometimes in person and always with well written documentation.

The next phase is negotiation with the selected candidate, the consultant acting as an objective professional third party. Then comes the resignation by the candidate after careful counseling by the consultant.

The consultant stays in close touch with candidate and client until the candidate is on board and for some time afterwards to help to ensure that any problems that may arise are successfully resolved.

Prior to recommending candidates, the consultant will have commenced checking on their backgrounds and reputations. Despite the difficulty of obtaining reliable information on an executive who is currently employed and whose candidacy must be kept secret, the consultant must obtain enough information about him to ensure that the client will not have any major unpleasant surprises later on regarding the candidate's past.

For most assignments, it is advisable to allow 45 days from the commencement of the search until the two or three candidates are formally presented to the client. More time for the search is usually needed when more than one country is involved. The period from presentation of candidates until the selected candidate is on board is influenced by many variables. Ideally, the interviews of candidates by the client plus the selection and negotiation process should take no more than a month, and the candidate should require no more than another month to extricate himself from his current position. Of course, contractual agreements between employer and executive sometimes result in a longer notice period.

F. How many executive search assignments are successful?

The one major underlying cause for the failure of executive search assignments is the lack of a sufficiently close partnership between search firm and client. To succeed, they must work closely together as a team. Failures will occur if the search firm does not carry out all of the steps thoroughly and professionally, and if the client does not provide the necessary information, handle candidates skillfully, conduct interviews promptly, and make decisions without delay. In fact, there is a direct relationship between the passage of time from the start of an assignment and the likelihood of failure.

Approximately 25% of all executive search assignments may not be completed successfully for reasons beyond the control of the search firm. Among these reasons are an unexpected change in the client organization structure, a sudden decision to promote from within because a previous internal candidate has changed his mind, or a change in the availability of an outside candidate who was previously under consideration.

What happens if an executive who has been placed by a search firm is terminated?

The fact is that the search firm has already expended the professional man-hours, has completed the assignment, and has been paid accordingly. As is true with other professions such as investment banking, law, and general management consulting, if the subsequent events bring negative results, the client is not entitled to any form of reimbursement. However, if the executive is terminated within twelve months of placement and if the reason for termination is clearly not the fault of the client, some search firms will make a special arrangement to replace the executive and bill the client for a partial service charge plus expenses.

G. What kinds of assignments are executive search firms most successful in completing?

The answer is that most kinds of upper-level executive search assignments can be successfully handled by a good search firm. If the search involves other countries, the firm should have proven experience in those countries. Success or failure is not governed so much by the kind of assignment but more on the selection of the right search firm and the establishment of a close working partnership beween client and search firm.

H. What is the present state of the executive search profession?

In the United States, there are a large number of executive search firms. To an increasing extent the responsibility for selecting search firms and overseeing their relationships with organizations has been delegated to senior personnel executives. Many of these personnel executives are thoroughly knowledgeable and highly selective.

Whereas many years ago only one search firm might be invited to discuss a confidential assignment, today it is not uncommon to have three or more search firms invited to make competitive presentations on a specific assignment.

To an increasing extent, these knowledgeable personnel executives have established detailed criteria for monitoring and assessing the performance of search firms. The line executives who are involved with the search participate in these assessments.

Concurrently, search firms are becoming more sophisticated. They are making increasing use of electronic data processing and are improving their research capability.

Executive search is not yet as well established as a profession as are law, banking, architecture, and engineering. But there are growing indications that executive search consultants, especially the more sophisticated ones, are now viewed as equally essential to the success of an enterprise as are the lawyers, the bankers, and the CPAs.

A good executive search firm can usually overcome most of the problems that make creative executive staffing so difficult. The professional executive search organization will more than justify its cost by being able to do well that which the organization cannot do as well itself.

I. What is the future outlook for the executive search profession?

During the next few years, we will probably see the continuing emergence of a few major strong executive search firms with worldwide coverage. Some smaller firms may well disappear as competition increases.

There will be increasing use made of electronic data processing and telecommunications. The next major area that is ripe for a breakthrough is in improving the ability of search firms to assess executives and predict their behavior and performance in relation to their client's needs.

Chapter Four

How to Select an Executive Search Firm

In preceding chapters we have discussed the decision-making process that finally leads to the conclusion that the services of an executive search firm are needed. Next comes the selection of the right firm.

In the United States, there are hundreds of search firms varying in size from one to over fifty consultants. In other countries, a similar variety of search firms has emerged on a smaller scale. Some firms own and directly control foreign affiliates while some others simply have agreements with firms abroad. Some search firms specialize in specific industries or functions or geographic areas while others are more generalized in the services that they offer.

The most comprehensive listing of executive search firms and executive recruiters appears in the *Directory of Executive Recruiters* published by *Consultants News*, Templeton Road, Fitzwilliam, N.H. 03447. *Executive Recruiter News*, a monthly publication by the same firm, provides current information.

Finding the firm that can provide optimum services for your specific requirements deserves substantial time and effort. Not only can the selection make the difference between success, mediocrity, or failure in solving your immediate executive staffing problem, but by establishing a close positive working partnership, you and the search firm will be ready to deal effectively with similar problems in the future.

The establishment of the general criteria to be used as a basis for your selection is the first step in the process.

The first and foremost of these criteria is the professional reputation of the search firm. This cannot be judged by the amount of publicity that the firm receives. It can only be determined by asking penetrating questions of executives whose judgment you trust in other companies who have retained search firms. Among these questions should be:

What search firms has your company used?

Why and how were they selected?

What work have these firms done for your company?

What degree of success did they have?

Within what time frame did they complete the work?

How did they charge for their services and expenses?

Were they thorough in their study of your problem, your organization, the position and the executive required to fill it?

Did they behave as professional consultants or only as order takers or headhunters?

How good is their judgment?

How many candidates did they recommend?

What is your opinion of the suitability of their candidates?

Were they energetic, dedicated, hard working?

Did they report progress to you weekly?

Did they try to push questionable candidates?

Did they level with you when they disagreed with your judgment?

How thorough was their background checking?

Did they assist you with selecting the successful candidate from among the finalists, with the negotiations, with extricating him from his company and bringing him aboard the company?

How effective was their overall management of the search as a project?

What is the name and position of the specific consultant in the search firm whom you would recommend?

If you had to fault them, what would be their weakness?

Have you had good reports on other search firms that you have not used?

If the position is an international one, geography is an essential criterion. Does the firm have the best capability to understand and handle an assignment that requires searching in other countries? You would probably not select a firm whose practice and whose consultants' backgrounds are limited to one country to undertake assignments involving one or more other countries.

Another criterion is organization level. Recruiting a Chief Executive Officer (CEO), an Executive Vice President, or the head of a large division might require a firm different from the one that you would select to recruit large numbers of senior professional technical personnel. For the senior levels, firms and consultants that are accustomed to working with top executives would be preferable, whereas the large numbers at lower levels require consultants who are experienced in handling projects of this nature.

To reduce the period required for the new executive to become effective, you may want him to come from your industry or a related industry. How much experience has the search firm had in that industry?

Does the firm have too many clients in your industry? Are they barred from searching among a high percentage of source companies? Professional search firms have limitations on taking executives away from their client companies.

To work with you effectively, a search consultant needs to become quite knowledgeable of your organization. Does his firm have a strict rule against using this information to recruit your executives? A search firm should not be expected to put your entire company off limits just because you have engaged them, for example, to fill a Finance Director position in one of your divisions. On the other hand, a professional search firm can be expected to make a commitment to you that they will not use any of the information that they obtain as a result of the client relationship with you to recruit executives from your company.

In one case, a search firm was retained locally by the General Manager in Venezuela to fill a Marketing Director position there. This was the only work that the firm had ever done for the company. At the same time, the firm persuaded that same company's General Manager in France to accept a position with another company in the same industry. The headquarters of the company with the Venezuela requirement complained to the search firm that they should not have taken one of their executives from anywhere in the world because the firm was working for that company in Venezuela. The search firm insisted that they had not behaved unethically because while working for that company's subsidiary in Venezuela, they had gained no knowledge or information whatsoever about their operations or executives in Europe.

Another criterion is the functional area. Does the firm have a successful record in completing assignments in the general management or marketing or finance or engineering or production or personnel functions, depending upon your requirement?

Another consideration is whether or not the firm has an office nearby, but it is not an important one. Certainly it is more convenient and possibly somewhat less expensive to work with a consultant in a nearby office, but this should only be a factor if the choice is between two or more firms of equal suitability, one of which has an office in your vicinity.

Having taken all of these steps and these criteria into consideration, you would by now have narrowed the selection to no more than three or four firms. Next comes meetings with these firms, which you can arrange either by calling the top man, or a particular consultant who has been recommended to you. Bear in mind that with increasing competition in the search profession, most firms have been improving their sales presentations. They are likely to be impressive. However, the quality of the presentation is not necessarily a reliable indication of the excellence of the service that you will get.

The firm's representatives should be carefully questioned, using all of the criteria suggested from the beginning of this chapter. Then comes a key point, Who would actually handle your assignment?

Some search firms have "front men" who are good salesmen and are mainly active in establishing and maintaining friendly relationships with clients, leaving the actual search work to less senior or even junior members of the firm. In other firms, the consultant to whom you give the assignment is the man who handles it. For international or foreign assignments, the consultant who is your main contact may have to utilize the services of offices in other parts of the world.

A major American consumer products company decided to overhaul its European operations. They made extensive inquiries in the U.S.A.

and Europe to obtain information about executive search firms with experience in Europe. As a result, they had meetings with five firms. One of these made an especially impressive presentation but was rejected when they could not satisfactorily answer some penetrating questions. In fact, the firm that was finally selected made no formal presentation at all, but was able to demonstrate a solid track record in Europe and to offer the services of consultants with long experience in that area.

It is essential for you to establish a clear understanding that there will be one consultant who is totally responsible to you for the successful completion of the assignment. Preferably, he will be the man who personally does the work. If other consultants have to share the work, whether they are in the same office or other offices or in other countries, you would be well advised to insist on a clear definition of the amount of control that your consultant has over the work to be done by others. The firm might be structured in such a way that every consultant has such a degree of independence that no one can cause him to be of much help to his partners. Foreign affiliations may be so loose that there is too little quality or other control between them. Then there is the overall complex problem of managing a search involving other consultants. Many consultants who function well on their own cannot manage a search in which others must participate, especially when they are in different countries.

Usually, a search in the United States ranges over many parts of the country. If both the client and the consultant are in New York and a prospective candidate is in Los Angeles, the client may demand, or the consultant may propose, that the candidate be interviewed by the consultant's Los Angeles office, thus saving the consultant's time and travel expense. But is this a wise decision? The consultant who is responsible for the assignment is in the best position to assess the suitability of a candidate and to compare him with other candidates. Therefore whether the search firm has one office or several offices in the U.S.A. is not nearly so important, when making your choice, as is the overall suitability of the firm and the consultant.

On the other hand, if you require a General Manager for your operations in Mexico or in Germany, for example, the main search would usually be conducted in the base country but would be extended beyond it to find executives who have backgrounds in the base country but who are located elsewhere. In these cases, you would be well advised to choose a firm that has an office in the base country, but you may elect to work with them through a consultant of the firm based in your own country; or you can establish a direct working arrangement with the consultant who is actually doing the work in the base country. Your choice would depend upon how well your local consultant knows your company, how many other executives at your headquarters are involved in the selection, and how often you travel to the country where the main search is being conducted.

All of these points are to be considered when selecting a search firm for a specific assignment and for a long-term relationship.

One multinational in the industrial products field has developed a highly successful relationship worldwide with an executive search firm. The Vice President Personnel together with the operating Vice President who is responsible for the area, decide whether the search firm is to be retained to solve a specific executive vacancy problem. If the position is at the country General Manager level, the Area Vice President is directly involved. For a position at, for example, the country Marketing Director or Financial Director level, the country General Manager and the search firm's managing partner in that country are the major members of the project team. A senior international consultant of the search firm in the U.S.A. maintains a close relationship with the Vice President Personnel, but also has access to the Area Vice President as required. The senior consultant in the U.S.A. ensures that the search is conducted effectively on a multicountry basis and handles communications with the company's headquarters.

An important consideration is how well the search firm is managed. Multi-office firms that achieve good teamwork are not plentiful. In some firms, where consultants are paid on the basis of their personal billings, they may be reluctant to share their clients, their assignments, or their billings. They may tend to overload so as to increase their billings. However, this does not necessarily mean that the firm and its consultants could not perform well for you. If these or any other search firms have effective leadership and management, their performance for you is likely to be good.

One major search firm solves this problem with a system of measuring and controlling the workloads of their consultants. During those periods when the search requires a substantial percentage of the consultant's time, the assignment is given a workload factor of three points. In the phase of the search mainly devoted to interviews by the client company and negotiations with the selected candidate, the workload factor may drop to two points. The final stage in which the consultant is maintaining contact with the candidate and the company while the candidate is resigning and settling in, may require a workload factor of only one point. By controlling the number of points that any consultant is permitted to carry, their workloads are kept within reasonable limits.

However, in making your selection, it is essential to ask penetrating questions about how the firm is managed, how quality is controlled, and what system, if any, exists to ensure that consultants are not overloaded. Satisfactory answers to your questions about teamwork are important, especially if more than one office of the search firm will be involved in the search.

One of the considerations in evaluating the suitability of a search firm and its teamwork is the research function. Usually, the research department manages the data system that contains the files on executives and on companies, plus a library of directories and other publications. Some research departments are limited to identifying prospective candidates, executives who could be sources of information, and companies in yours and related industries, together with information on their executives. Other research departments go further and do much of the search work by contacting the sources and the prospective candidates themselves, with the objective of presenting to the consultant a list of candidates to be interviewed.

There are two problems with research departments of which you should be aware when selecting a search firm. One is that they often become bottlenecks so that a month or more may go by before the consultant obtains the information that he needs. The other problem is that the lazy or overloaded consultant becomes too dependent on the research department. As a result, he lacks the comprehensive and profound knowledge that is essential to the excellent performance of his role.

In one search firm, the consultant does not start to work on the search until the research department presents to him a list of candidates to be interviewed.

In another search firm, there is no research department. The only data available to the consultants are a computerized listing of executives on file and the folders containing the details of past searches. In a third firm, the research department works closely with the consultant in developing information that enables the consultant to expedite the search. All three firms do good work because of the quality of their consultants and their management.

Time frame is another important factor. Generally speaking, the best work is done on a search while it is still new and fresh. If it drags on, creativity and quality usually suffer. The search firm that commences a major effort on the same day that they accept an assignment is more likely to succeed than is the firm that delays or starts slowly. You should obtain commitments on weekly reporting to you by the consultant and an understanding that the two or three or four candidates who are to be seriously considered by you will be presented within 45 days of the commencement of the assignment. If the search is worldwide, more than 45 days may be necessary.

Finally, in making your selection, you would be well advised to use, as a guide, the following Code of Ethics of the Association of Executive Search Consultants.

Code of ethics
I. Professionalism

Executive search consulting is a professional endeavor. A profession is characterized by the objectivity, integrity, and thoroughness of its practitioners. Members will maintain the highest standards of professional work and behavior so that their actions reflect favorably on the association, its members, and their clients and candidates. In this endeavor, members will serve their clients in a professional manner, including the performance of at least the following services before proposing any candidates:

    a. Meetings with the client to develop understanding of the client's organization and needs and the position to be filled

    b. Written documentation outlining the position description, scope, and character of the services to be provided

    c. Thorough independent research on the nature and needs of the client organization

    d. Comprehensive search for qualified candidates

    e. Thorough evaluation of potential candidates, including in-depth personal interviews, verification of credentials, and careful assessment of the individual's strengths and weaknesses, in order to provide an adequate basis for independent and expert recommendations to the client

    f. Either before or after presentation of a candidate, but prior to final selection by the client, performance of comprehensive reference checking

Any practices that do not embody the above process cannot be objective, are adverse to the client's best interest, undermine independent judgment, tend to bring disrepute to the profession, and are in violation of this code.

II. Qualifications

Members will accept only those assignments that they are qualified to undertake on the basis of full knowledge of the client situation and the professional competence and capacity of the consultants involved. Assignments accepted will be based on a comprehensive written document outlining the scope and character of the services to be provided.

III. Client relationship*

Members will, in each assignment undertaken, define in writing what constitutes "the client organization." The member will not recruit or cause to be recruited any person from the defined client organization for a period of two years after the completion of such assignment unless the member firm and client agree in writing to an exception. The member will disclose to the client limitations arising through service to other clients that may affect the scope of the search assignment. In the event that a client retains a member to conduct a search and any other firm has already been retained by the client, the member shall assure that its retention is fully disclosed to such other previously retained firms.

IV. Confidentiality

Members shall regard as totally confidential all information concerning the business affairs of their clients and of candidates.

V. Promotion activities

Members will conduct all firm promotion, public relations, and new business activities in a manner that involves no representations, express

---

*This section of the Code of Ethics is the subject of disagreement among many of the best executive search firms that maintain high ethical standards. Many insist that to be able to provide top service to all of their clients, they must be free to exercise judgment as to the degree of protection that they will grant to each client and that the degree will change according to circumstances.

or implied, that are false, deceptive, unsubstantiated, or that otherwise have a capacity to mislead.

VI. Promotion of competition

It is the policy of AESC and its members to promote free and fair competition in the provision of executive recruiting consulting services. Neither AESC nor any member will engage in any unlawful restraint of trade, unfair method of competition, or other violation of the antitrust laws.

It does not matter whether the firm that you select belongs to the Association of Executive Search Consultants. What does matter is whether the firm adheres to these professional practices.

As important as all of these criteria are, the overriding ones are the reputation of the firm and the track record and personality of the consultants who will be responsible for handling your assignments. Keep in mind, during the selection process, that your objective is to find a search firm and one or more consultants within that firm with whom you can establish a close working partnership that will produce optimum results for you.

In the United States, there are two good listings of search firms. The more comprehensive of these is the *Directory of Executive Recruiters,* published by Consultants News, Templeton Road, Fitzwilliam, N.H. 03447. The other is the Association of Executive Search Consultants from which a list of member firms can be obtained. Their address is: 151 Railroad Avenue, Greenwich, Conn. 06830. You can keep abreast of current information on search firms by subscribing to *Executive Recruiter News,* published by Kennedy & Kennedy, Inc., Templeton Road, Fitzwilliam, N.H. 03447.

Chapter Five

How Much Should You Pay an Executive Search Firm?

In other chapters, the difference between an executive recruiting firm that charges for its services on a contingent basis and an executive search firm that works on a retainer basis has been discussed. Briefly, a client is only obligated to pay a contingent firm if the firm places a candidate with the client company, whereas an executive search firm is retained and is paid on a current basis for the work that it does.

It is inadvisable to retain a search firm just to find a qualified executive. Search firms are retained to help you to develop the best solution to an executive vacancy problem. The search firm's services can be measured on the basis of its overall contribution to the solution of that problem whether or not the end result is the replacement of an executive who has been recommended by the search firm.

To understand the reasons for the methods of charging that are utilized by an executive search firm, some knowledge of their operating expenses and financial management can be helpful. To provide consistently good service, a search firm must have good executives. As in every other business and profession, effective executives command high compensation. On average, each executive search assignment requires about 150 man-hours of professional time apart from the basic supporting staff services. A search firm usually maintains a research staff and facilities, an electronic data processing system, an accounting organization, top-notch secretarial staff, highly competent filing, switchboard, and receptionist personnel, word processing equipment, and attractive office space. In addition, there is heavy long-distance telephone and telex expense, substantial travel, and the costs of numerous breakfasts, lunches, and dinners with sources and prospective candidates.

To attract and retain good professionals, a search firm must pay them between 40% and 60% of the firm's service billings, depending upon whether the professionals are shareholders who benefit from share appreciation realized from retained earnings. Therefore, the search firm must produce a constant stream of sufficient income to maintain its staff and pay its expenses.

Recruiting firms that work on a contingent basis are forced to concentrate on placing as many executives as possible at least cost. This is why they have a tendency to overwhelm clients with quantities of résumés. They cannot afford to risk 150 professional man-hours on an assignment, not knowing whether they will earn a single dollar for their efforts. To perform as a truly professional executive search consultant, he and his firm must be retained so that they are being paid for their services and reimbursed for their expenses no matter whether they place a candidate with their client.

In other chapters, the importance of a positive partnership between client and search firm is emphasized. When this is achieved, the client is kept fully informed of progress and has every opportunity to participate in the entire process. Under these circumstances, the chances of failing to successfully solve the client's problem are minimized. However, there are a number of circumstances that may result in the client's problem being solved without a candidate being placed by the search firm. Here are some examples:

An internal candidate may surface unexpectedly.

An internal candidate who previously rejected the opportunity may suddenly change his mind and decide to accept the position. This may be true also of an outside candidate who was previously contacted directly by the client and who rejected the opportunity and subsequently changed his mind.

Companies sometimes have a search conducted so that they can compare outside executives with their own internal candidates.

After they have discussed several prospects and seriously considered two or three candidates, they may decide that the position should be offered to their internal candidate.

Developments may occur, such as a change in business plans, a government decree, a sudden downturn in the economy, or a reorganization, any of which can cause the client to suspend or cancel the assignment.

Search firms could not survive under these circumstances if they were not paid for the substantial work that they have done on assignments that are cancelled for reasons beyond their control. It is for such reasons that search firms charge retainers. Usually these retainers are credited against a basic charge. The basic charge is calculated either as a percentage of the annual compensation required to attract a qualified candidate or as a fixed amount based upon the estimated difficulty of solving the client's problem. When a percentage is applied, it usually ranges between 30% and 35% of the annual compensation required to attract the right executive. Either 30% or 33⅓% are extensively applied when the search is confined to one major country such as the United States, Mexico, or Germany or a group of small countries such as Benelux. Most firms have a minimum basic charge that is based upon approximately one third of the bottom end of the salary range of the lowest level position for which they will consider searching.

If a multicountry search is needed, many firms charge 35% and in some cases more. The multicountry search involves a basic problem with the economics of the project. For example, a search for a Vice President International to be responsible worldwide for all operations outside the United States necessitates searching everywhere in the world where qualified candidates might be found. Usually such a search is given to a firm that has offices around the world, and the consultants in those offices are expected to participate in the search.

Obviously, such an undertaking requires substantially more manhours than would normally be the case where only one country need be considered. On the other hand, there is usually resistance by clients to paying more than 35% for an international search. The problem is exacerbated by the fact that most international search firms, when competing to obtain the assignment, will offer worldwide search services at somewhere between 30% and 35%. The fact is that no search firm can afford to conduct a thorough search in every major country around the world while charging no more than 35%. Either they must take shortcuts or decide to absorb the loss in order to obtain or maintain the client relationship. If a thorough search in many countries is truly justified, it would be wiser for the client to reach an understanding with the search firm on a special basis for payment of services, realistically related to the effort required.

The retainers charged by search firms are established in a variety of ways. They are usually related to the basic charge. Many firms bill on a "⅓, ⅓, ⅓" basis. The first ⅓ of the estimated basic charge may be billed at the outset of the assignment or at the end of the first month, the second ⅓ a month later, and the final ⅓ either a month after that or when the assignment is successfully completed. Other firms charge ⅕ at the outset and ⅕ each month until the assignment is completed or the estimated basic charge has been reached, whichever comes first. There are other variations. There is often a differential charge to be paid when the assignment is completed because the basic charge ends up being somewhat higher than the total of the retainers that have been paid.

Most, but not all search firms charge out-of-pocket expenses. They also charge for the travel expenses incurred for interviewing prospective candidates. The out-of-pocket expenses include long-distance and telex charges, as well as meals with prospective candidates and sources. For a search in one country, these out-of-pocket expenses might average 500 dollars per month, but if the search is multicountry, the expenses can go far beyond this figure. Any expensive travel is usually discussed with the client before it is undertaken. While there is certainly no excuse for charging exorbitant expenses, it is advisable to keep in mind that if you are too tough with the search firm about its expenses, you may be inhibiting thorough search work.

At least one firm charges additionally for the work done by its research team. Their rationale is that they could not afford to maintain such a top notch team without charging extra for its services. They also point out that there is a great variation in the amount of research service required for different assignments and that their clients are charged according to the actual man-hours devoted to research in each case.

The heaviest expenditure of man-hours by a search firm usually occurs during the first four to six weeks of the assignment. It is for this reason that most firms have established a system of charging retainers so that a substantial proportion of the estimated basic charge is billed during the first few weeks. It may be argued that this procedure can result in almost all of the basic charge being paid to the firm before the assignment is successfully completed and that therefore they have little incentive to continue their work beyond that point. The fact is that a good search firm gains and maintains its reputation and image through satisfied clients. Reputation is by far the major incentive for continuing to work hard with the client whether or not most or all of the basic charge has already been billed.

Should special payment arrangements be made when the company has several similar positions to fill?

For example, a client decides to overhaul its marketing organization worldwide and concludes that many of the Marketing Directors of their subsidiaries in the U.S. and around the world must be replaced. The specification requires that candidates must be executives who are transferable from one country to another. In such cases, agreement is often reached on a modest reduction in the basic charge and the retainers. The reductions are usually based on the search firm's best estimate of the decrease in the man-hours required to complete each assignment successfully because of the opportunity to work on several similar requirements at the same time.

Questions that are frequently asked about retainer arrangements are: What if we cancel the assignment? What if the assignment continues beyond the point at which the retainers that have already been billed equal the basic charge? What if the specifications for the assignment are substantially changed during the search? What if, after working on the assignment for an extraordinarily long period, the search firm is still unable to complete it successfully? What if the position is filled by an executive who is not developed by the search firm? What if the executive who is placed with us leaves our company?

If an assignment is cancelled for internal reasons by the client, the only obligation to the search firm is to pay the retainer on a prorated basis up to the date of cancellation. When work is prolonged by the client because of their inability to meet interview schedules or due to delays in making decisions, a special arrangement is usually made with the search firm to continue paying the retainer beyond the amount of the basic charge, possibly at a somewhat reduced rate.

When there is a substantial change in the specifications during the search, this often requires that the search firm start all over again. In that case, it is only fair that an agreement is reached whereby the search firm is compensated for the additional effort that will be needed. Under some such circumstances, the retainer payment schedule is started all over again from scratch with no credit to the client for retainers billed up until the time of the change. In most cases, however, a compromise is agreed upon whereby part of the retainer due up to the point of the change is credited to the new search.

If an assignment is not completed, the settlement of payment for services depends upon circumstances. Responsibility for the results of an executive search assignment must be shared by both the search firm and the client. If the search firm is partially at fault, they should admit it and arrange to credit their client with part of the retainer against a future assignment.

If the position is filled by an executive other than one found by the executive search firm, settlement of payment again depends upon circumstances. As stated at the beginning of this chapter, an executive search firm is retained to solve a problem involving an executive vacancy and not just to find a qualified executive. It frequently happens that during the course of the search, the client learns about candidates from other sources. The best practice is to refer these candidates to the search firm to be evaluated alongside those that have been discovered as a result of the search. If one of these referred candidates is selected, the search firm can continue to provide its normal services during the negotiation, resignation, and indoctrination phases and be paid as if the candidate had been discovered by the search firm. This way of handling such situations eliminates the undesirable consequences of the search firm's feeling that they are competing with the client, and it encourages the search firm to judge all candidates from whatever source on an objective basis.

When an executive who has been placed by a search firm leaves the client company, the search firm can insist that it has already done the work that was required to find and install the executive. The client company would, therefore, be obligated to pay the entire cost of another search assignment to replace the departed executive. However, most search firms, being conscious of the importance of an ongoing positive relationship with their clients, will negotiate a mutually acceptable arrangement for the replacement of the lost executive, especially if the loss occurs within a year of the date that the executive joined the company.

In summary, it bears repetition to point out that achieving the best possible service from an executive search firm requires a close positive partnership between the consultant and the client. When this partnership relationship is achieved, there are usually few if any problems related to payments for services and expenses because there is a thorough understanding and appreciation of each other's roles, of the method of charging for services and of the work done.

Chapter Six

Working with Your Executive Search Firm Before the Search Begins

Now that you have selected the executive search firm with which you are going to work to solve your problem, there are seven steps that should be taken. The objective of these steps is to provide a sound basis for the close working relationship or the partnership beween you and the search firm that is essential to success. There will be a direct relationship between the outcome of your project and the care and attention that are given to these steps.

Step no. 1. Appointment of the consultant

The first step has been discussed in Chapter Four. It consists of having a clear understanding regarding the specific individual consultant of the search firm who is responsible for handling your assignment. There should be agreement on what his role will be, i.e., is he to be, in effect, a project manager, assisted by other consultants in the firm or will he perform most of the work himself? What, precisely, will be the role of the search firm's research department? Will they be providers of data to the consultant, or will they, in addition, be participating in the search by contacting sources and prospective candidates? For the most senior-level positions, some companies prefer that sources and prospective candidates are contacted only by consultants rather than by researchers.

If the search is to be transnational, what will be the involvement of the search firm's other offices and who will be responsible for their performance? In any case, it is essential that one consultant is clearly responsible for your assignment. He must be someone to whom you and your colleagues can relate well and in whom you have confidence.

Step no. 2. Appointment of the responsible executive in your company

The second step is mainly concerned with your own organization. There should be an executive in your company who is responsible for the search assignment and the main relationship with the search firm. The other executives in your firm who will interview candidates or who will be involved otherwise in decisions that will have to be made before the candidate is in place should be clearly designated.

Step no. 3. Creation of a partnership between you and your search firm

A key to success in working with a search firm is a close, positive, working relationship. At the outset, the aim should be to create, informally, a sense of partnership between your company and your search firm. The third step is the establishment of an agreement on how the partnership between your company and the search firm will function. A typical agreement would stipulate that the main stream of communications will flow between the consultant in charge of the assignment and the company executive who has been made responsible for the assignment. If there are to be communications with other executives in your company or with other consultants in the search firm, perhaps in offices in other countries, these arrangements should be spelled out.

In one case, after the search was well under way for a General Manager to take charge of Benelux operations, the search firm was caught in the cross fire between the Corporate Vice President Personnel based in New York and the Area Vice President based in Europe. Both were insisting that the main stream of communications regarding the search and prospective candidates should be directed to each of them. The resulting confusion and friction greatly prolonged the assignment and caused the loss of promising candidates.

The billing procedure should be clearly agreed upon so that it is unlikely that there will be misunderstandings regarding the amounts to be billed for services and expenses, the timing of the bills, and to whom invoices are to be sent. This latter point is especially important in view of the confidentiality of most executive search assignments.

There was a recent case in which the billing process was not clearly spelled out. The executive to be replaced was the Senior Vice President Finance, but he had not been informed of the decision to terminate him. A letter from the search firm confirming the conditions under which they were undertaking the assignment, and to which the first invoice was attached, was addressed to the Chief Executive Officer (CEO). The CEO's secretary was on vacation and her stand-in, trying to follow instructions to screen the heavy flow of paper coming into the CEO's office, upon seeing that this particular letter had an invoice attached to it, referred it to the Senior Vice President Finance. The CEO will never forget the resulting embarrassment and repercussions.

Step no. 4. Development of a clear understanding of the specifications

The fourth step deserves substantial time and careful thought. It consists of developing a clear and comprehensive understanding of all aspects of this particular executive search project. The chances of filling your executive vacancy successfully are directly related to how well both you and the consultant understand the entire problem and the degree to which you are in agreement. To achieve this common understanding, here is a listing of the information that will be needed:

A. The company and the position

What are the objectives of your company? How well are they being achieved?

What are the basic statistics of your entire company and that part of your company to which the open position belongs, such as historical information, plant and office locations, affiliations, product lines, sales volume, share of market, profitability, number and classifications of employees, past, current, and projected rates of growth?

What are the reasons for the existence of the open position? Why does it have to be filled? What are all the circumstances surrounding the vacating of the position by the executive who occupied it?

Why is the position not being filled by an executive who is currently with the company?

What efforts have been made, so far, to fill the position?

What are the short-range and long-range plans of the company that would affect the future incumbent?

What objectives will the new person be expected to achieve, over what period?

What specific results must he produce? Within what time frames?

What are the specific authorities, responsibilities, accountabilities, functions, and duties of the open position? The answers to this question should include an organization chart of the entire company plus a more detailed chart together with position descriptions of those parts of the organization that directly concern the open position—above, below, and at the same level, including functional as well as direct relationships.

How do the informal organizations within the company operate? How are they likely to affect the new executive?

Every company has a personality, idiosyncracies, formal and informal policies, practices, and rules. All of these that would influence the selection of the candidate should be spelled out.

What are the strengths and weaknesses of the company and of that part of the organization with which the candidate will be mainly involved?

What are the distinctive personality and behavior traits of the executives in the company with whom the selected candidate will work?

What will be your answer when candidates ask, "What would be the future opportunities for me in your company?"

B. The candidate

There are numerous true stories with the following basic theme. An executive search firm undertakes an assignment to fill a senior-level position reporting to the President of the client company. The specifications are extremely tough. The consultant and his partners spend an extraordinary amount of time trying to find and interest the unique individual demanded by the President. Finally, they succeed in developing two candidates who meet the specifications and who are willing to explore the opportunity. At this point, the President informs the consultant that he has found and hired an executive for the open position. When he identifies the executive, the search firm is shocked because most of the specifications that made the search so difficult were disregarded in the President's selection.

There is a tendency to go to extremes in establishing specifications by which candidates are to be judged. Too often, they are either excessive or superficial. To obtain the best results, it is essential that candidate specifications be specific, practical, and comprehensive.

There are always certain requirements that absolutely must be met. They are essential to the successful performance of the job. These should be clearly identified as essentials. In addition, there are numerous desirable specifications that when added to the essentials, could increase the candidate's effectiveness on the job. These should be clearly labeled as desired but not essential so that they do not distract everyone from giving full weight to the essentials. For example, must the candidate have an MBA or a Ph.D. or a CPA or would a proven successful record make these desirable but not essential? Must the executive have already achieved Chief Executive Officer level or could he, at present, be a promising number two? The point is that by making sure that the essentials are clearly defined and described, the likelihood of finding and attracting the right person is greatly enhanced.

Continuing with the questions that need to be answered: What educational background is essential for this position? What alternatives would be acceptable? What additional educational qualifications would be desirable?

Specifically, what experience is essential to enable an executive to achieve the objectives and meet the desired performance standards for this position? In addition to the most obvious requirements, how well must the executive be qualified in other areas of management? What additional experience would be desirable? Industries, product lines, markets, functions, and geographic areas all need to be considered. The required experience should be described so thoroughly that there will be no misunderstanding.

Such statements as "must have held senior-level financial position in a medium-sized company for at least five years" are superficial and inadequate. Specifically what responsibilities must the executive have had? In what size and types of companies? In what functional areas must this individual be especially strong? Is international experience essential or desirable? If so, specifically what experience and in which geographic areas? For example, for a financial position, should the executive come from companies in which the reporting relationship between levels in the financial organization equals that of the line organization?

For positions of international responsibility, proven ability to function well in the culture systems encompassed by the vacant position is important. Language requirements must be carefully considered.

To what extent does the spouse become a factor in the position to be filled? The role of the spouse should not be overlooked, especially if the position is in a foreign country or in a smaller community.

How would you describe the personality of the executive who would be most likely to succeed in this position? For example, does it require a highly creative dynamo, or a calm, steady, hands-on, good manager? Is an entrepreneurial type needed or is the position one that is best occupied by an executive who will skillfully manage an existing organization? How important are appearance, presence, interpersonal relationship skills, and team work?

The term "best" is too often misused in describing the desired executive. The "best in his field" is not always the right man and tends to be confused with "best for this position." For example, a General Manager with a strong marketing background may insist upon the best Marketing Director in the industry. The best is hired, and they clash. The new executive is out within six months. The General Manager was unwilling to delegate the marketing responsibility, but this fact was not thrashed out before the search was undertaken.

In another case, much time and effort were wasted because of a division head insisting upon recruiting the "best" research and development executive in the industry. In fact, what was needed was an effective manager of applications engineering. Research and development was ably conducted by the parent company. Only after every potential candidate who met the original specification rejected the job, did the division head face reality and adjust the specifications accordingly.

The objective is to recruit the best executive for the position. He may not have to be the best in the industry or in his profession, but he will almost certainly be one of the top performers with a background that fits the specifications.

Integrity is an absolute essential in every executive position. It should be included in the specification so that it will not be overlooked.

Finally, two lists should be made. The first list should identify those companies that would be the most suitable sources of executives to fill the vacant position. The second list should specify companies that, for whatever reason, must be off-limits as sources for your requirement.

An executive search firm that is retained by an organization is acting as a representative of that organization. Therefore, the search firm must comply with the Equal Employment Opportunity law. There must be no discrimination in selecting candidates because of their sex, race, religion, or age.

C. Compensation

The compensation part of the position specification is too often treated superficially. As this is usually a complex and often emotional subject that directly influences the degree of success of the search, it merits thorough treatment.

There are frequently four major hurdles in deciding upon the compensation package to be offered. One of these is the data obtained through surveys. When the survey indicates that the average range for the position is $100,000 to $150,000 salary plus bonus, should you assume that you can attract the right executive at the $100,000 level? The answer depends upon the other parts of the specifications. If you are seeking a Division General Manager and if you insist that candidates must currently be Division General Managers of similar operations, then you are unlikely to attract good candidates at the bottom end of the scale. If you have decided that you must have the best Division General Manager in your industry, you will probably have to be prepared to offer substantially more than the maximum of the range because the best is probably already at or above the average maximum. On the other hand, if you decide that you would be better off to bring in a good number two from a similar division in another company, you may be able to attract the executive at or near the bottom of the average range.

Another hurdle, if you want the best in the industry, is your own internal compensation structure. If, to attract a top candidate, you must offer substantially more than the approved internal range, can you justify reevaluation of the position or acceptance of a compensation level above the range? If the new executive is brought in at the top of or above the approved range, how can the compensation be adjusted upwards in the future?

A third hurdle is the rest of the compensation package. These include items such as deferred compensation, loans, profit sharing, stock options, savings plans, life, medical, accident, and disability insurances, pension plans, clubs, chauffeurs, automobiles, vacations, allowances, expenses, and reimbursements for moving from one location to another. If the position is overseas, the various foreign-service allowances, housing, schooling, home leave, tax equalization, currencies, and locations from which compensation is paid are among the additional subjects to be decided. Added to these are other special perquisites and privileges that are often provided. In its totality, this part of the compensation package sometimes carries more weight than the salary and bonus in attracting the right man. Therefore, it is wise to decide in advance how much flexibility there would be in offering to compensate a candidate for losses such as vesting rights, stock options, and deferred compensation and in offsetting benefits, perquisites, and privileges that he currently enjoys that may not be available in your company. Finally, the bottom lines, after taxes, need to be compared.

At the more senior levels and for some professional technical positions, up-front bonuses are sometimes paid to candidates upon acceptance of the position. These bonuses often serve two purposes. They tip the scale in favor of making the move. They sometimes reduce the amount of salary that has to be offered, thus easing the strain on the salary structure.

Related to the compensation package is the question of moving costs. Are you aware of and prepared to underwrite all of the costs and expenses involved in moving an executive and his family from one location to another?

The fourth hurdle concerns the degree of confidence that you have in your search firm. The consultant has two incentives to make the compensation package richer. One is that he can more easily attract good executives. Secondly, his service charge is usually based upon the cash part of the package—the higher the salary and bonus paid to the successful candidate, the greater, usually, is the amount earned by the search firm.

A truly professional executive search consultant will exclude these two factors entirely from his thinking. His sole objective will be to help you to solve your problem as effectively as possible. If you have selected a true professional, you can rely heavily on his guidance in establishing the compensation package.

To summarize, the compensation package and the rest of the specifications for the assignment have to be in balance. If you insist upon specifications at the 99th percentile you will almost certainly have to pay a substantial premium. If you are not prepared to pay the premium, the specifications will have to be adjusted so that you can offer a package that is sufficiently attractive without severely straining your company's compensation practices and structure.

Step no. 5. Agreement on a timetable

The fifth step is the determination of a timetable. Of course an executive search project involves too many variables to permit precise timing, but there should be agreement on the approximate programming of the basic steps. It is usually advisable to ask the consultant in charge to report progress weekly beginning with the first week. For most assignments, with the exception of those requiring multicountry searching, all of the candidates should have been presented within a period of 45 days.

A thorough search is hard work, and it is very time-consuming. If you apply too much pressure in an effort to accelerate the presentation of candidates, you may cause the consultant to take short cuts that would reduce your chances of bringing in the optimum candidate. On the other hand, when you reach the stage of interviewing candidates, a real effort should be made to confine to one month the period during which candidates are being considered by the company and the selection decision is being made. To the extent that this process goes beyond one month, the risk of losing good candidates is greatly increased.

Step no. 6. Review of Executives who have already been considered

An essential ingredient of an effective partnership between the search firm and the client is complete frankness and confidence. As has been previously emphasized, the objective of the partnership is to develop the best solution to your problem.

Before the search gets started, the consultant should be thoroughly briefed on all prospective candidates, internal and external, who have been considered, with explanations as to why they have not been recruited for the position. Not only does this provide valuable insights into your company's thinking about candidates for the position, but it ensures that the consultant will not waste his time with these executives.

Such questions need to be answered as: Are any of these former prospective candidates still under consideration? If so, what is the search consultant's relationship with them to be? What if an executive who has rejected the position changes his mind?

Some companies take the position that if an executive who has not been found by the search firm is hired for the vacant position, the search firm will only be paid for its services up to the date that it is notified that the search is terminated.

Other companies take quite a different approach. They retain the search firm to help them to solve the problem, and if it is solved successfully, the search firm will be paid the full service charge, no matter who found the candidate. They point out that this approach enables them to request the search firm to apply its talents and services to selection from among, and negotiations with, all potential candidates, no matter from what source. The consultant may well succeed in persuading an internal candidate to change his mind. He may do the same with an external candidate who has rejected the position. The search firm is not made to feel that it has to compete with its client in an effort to place one of the search firm's candidates in the position.

This latter approach is much more likely to produce the best results. After all, you should not be paying a search firm simply to find a qualified executive. To obtain full value, you should retain the firm's total professional competence to achieve the best solution to your executive vacancy problem. That problem is usually not solved until the right man or woman is in place and functioning effectively.

Step no. 7. Preparation of written position description

The final step, before the search begins, is the preparation of a comprehensive written description. All of the information that has been developed throughout the previous six steps will be included. The description is normally drafted by the consultant, discussed with you, and then written in final form.

Most executive search assignments are urgent. There are, at times, situations in which travel schedules make it impractical to discuss the draft position description before the search begins. Under such circumstances, common sense indicates that the search should start without delay and the paper work be completed as soon as possible.

Speaking of common sense and urgency, the head of a search firm had just completed giving an intensive training course to a new consultant. Most of Sunday had been spent on the steps described in this chapter. On Monday morning the new consultant began the period of observing the head of the firm in action.

An urgent phone call came in from the President of one of the firm's major clients. The President was at the airport about to depart on a three week business trip to Europe. He told the head of the search firm that they had lost a Division General Manager and had just decided to go outside the company for his replacement. The conversation lasted about three minutes, as the President's flight was being called. He told the head of the search firm to proceed immediately on an urgent basis.

The new consultant was, of course, dumbfounded. How could the head of the firm, after having insisted upon thoroughness in all of these steps, accept a new assignment on the basis of a three minute telephone conversation?

The fact was that a close, long-standing relationship existed between the company and the search firm. The President could be confident that the right consultant would be assigned and that the assignment would be given the usual professional and urgent attention. The search firm had most of the information needed for the search. Common sense indicated that the search could and should start immediately.

Chapter Seven

Working with Your Executive Search Firm During the Actual Search

Now that there is a clear understanding, in writing, between you and your executive search consultant on all aspects of the position to be filled, on the executive to be found, and on the conditions under which the entire project will be handled, the next phase—the search—can begin. It is in this phase that the importance of the close working partnership between you and the consultant will become more evident.

Both of you are embarking upon a very complex mission. The objective of the mission is to find and install that special individual, among the dozens or hundreds that may be qualified on paper, who is most likely to produce the desired results for you.

This search phase of the project will usually require about six weeks. The research; the systematic contacting of sources, i.e., those people who are knowledgeable of executives in the industry, function, and geographic areas that are your targets; the approaching and screening of possible candidates; and the interviewing of prospective candidates requires well over 100 man-hours of well-organized, intensive work. These man-hours have to be spread over a period of several weeks because the process requires waiting time to make contacts, to obtain responses from the scores of people with whom the consultant must communicate, and to arrange interviews. When the search encompasses several countries, the man-hours and the time span increase. A worldwide search may require ten or twelve weeks.

When a worldwide or multicountry search is required, the consultant in charge of the project has, in addition to the search process, a difficult management responsibility. He must ensure that his fellow consultants in his firm's offices in other countries have a thorough knowledge of the client organization and the position to be filled and that they clearly understand the specifications of the executive for whom they are searching. He must ensure that their responses are timely. He must evaluate the data that they send to him by mail, telex, and telephone and respond to them promptly. He has to exercise judgment on their recommendations.

It is wise for you to arrange with your consultant to call you at least once each week, beginning with the first week, to discuss progress. Your consultant will probably be handling five or six other assignments at various stages of completion. He might be tempted to give more attention to those with which he is experiencing time pressure instead of to your brand-new search. If you and he let two or three weeks slip by without much action, your consultant will subsequently have to try to play catch-up, and that can lead to shortcuts that adversely affect quality.

When you arrange for the weekly report, it is essential that you plan to make yourself readily available to receive or return your consultant's calls. A major cause of problems between organizations and search firms is inadequate communication. It is difficult enough to summarize progress on a complex search and to describe and discuss executives. The problem is compounded if your consultant has to struggle to reach you, and if you are under time pressure when he finally makes contact with you.

Executives who have had little experience with executive search often exclaim "that one will be a breeze!" when a vacancy is to be filled. Even mature consultants sometimes make this mistake. Experience teaches that the easy executive search assignments are almost nonexistent. It is true that on very rare occasions, the ideal executive is found in the files or in the consultant's memory bank, recommended, and hired within days after the search begins. Such events are the result of a combination of unusual circumstances and luck. The attendant publicity gives the false impression that these quick solutions occur far more often than is actually the case.

For example, suppose that you have arranged with your executive search consultant to fill your vacant Vice President Finance position. On the surface, it might appear that this ought to be an easy one. After all, there are thousands of qualified financial executives in the United States. A good search firm already has a fair percentage of these executives in their data system. Through directories, a substantial additional number can be identified before any "sourcing" begins. So you might well assume that it should be a simple matter for your consultant, within a few days, to quickly select two or three of these executives and present them as prospective candidates. The experienced search consultant knows better.

His mission is to help you to fill the position with an executive who has the best overall qualifications in terms of professional background, experience, and personality for your particular requirements. This means that the consultant cannot be sure that he is fulfilling his part of the mission unless his search has included consideration of so many possible candidates that he is confident that the two or three whom he finally recommends are among the best-qualified executives who can be found for your vacancy. Both you and the consultant have to be confident that it is unlikely that there are better executives who could be attracted to this particular position.

This is one of the essential differences between the executive recruiter or headhunter and the executive search consultant. A recruiter or headhunter is simply that. His mission is to find someone who is qualified—never mind whether the candidate is among the best that can be found for your particular position. It is the added dimension of finding and filling the position with the best-qualified executive that is part of the reason for paying retainers to a search consultant rather than a "finder's fee" to a recruiter or headhunter.

Returning to the example of the Vice President Finance position, the executive search consultant, as already indicated, would begin the search by having the data researched that is immediately available within his firm. In addition, he will have obtained from you lists of financial executives whom you know and of companies whose quality of financial management you admire. The search firm's records will include financial executives who have been interviewed or contacted for similar positions, files on prior similar searches, résumés, and a variety of directories. The results of the research will provide the consultant with several categories of information. First there will usually be a list of qualified executives who are known to consultants in the firm or to executives in your company. A second much longer list will include executives in the firm's files and your company's files who are unknown to you or any of the consultants. An even longer third list will include names, titles, and companies obtained from various directories. A fourth list would consist of executives who could be good sources of information for this particular search but who would not themselves be potential candidates.

With this array of data, consisting of dozens up to hundreds of names, the consultant decides on a strategy that will enable him to find, with optimum efficiency, the three best possible candidates for your Vice President Finance position. Concurrently, he will probably have a brainstorming session with his fellow consultants to help to ensure that he has developed the best strategy and has not overlooked any prospective candidates who might be suggested by consultants in the firm.

At this point the consultant will commence the sifting of the data. He will eliminate from further consideration those people who, although qualified, do not come close enough to the ideal that is being sought. This step reduces the pool of possible candidates substantially.

At this stage, the consultant will usually divide his time between studying in more detail the data on those executives whose backgrounds appear to be a possible fit and contacting sources who have a wide knowledge of the industries and the profession in which the search is being conducted. Continuing with this division of time, the consultant will try to select two or three files on executives whose backgrounds appear to be right and, without identifying them, he will discuss them with you informally. This is somewhat like the custom tailor showing you some samples of cloth and suits after you have described your requirements, so that he can obtain a clearer idea of your tastes and preferences. This process of discussing "samples" is usually quite rewarding because it clarifies and sometimes alters the thinking about the person who would be most likely to succeed in the position.

In the meantime, your consultant is gathering information from his sources. They are suggesting prospective candidates and are answering his numerous questions about executives on his lists whose backgrounds appear to fit the essentials.

All of these activities will bring your consultant to the point at which he begins to contact prospective candidates on whom he has obtained enough information to convince him that they are qualified. Many of them will immediately either eliminate themselves or be eliminated by the consultant for a variety of reasons such as a recent promotion, family would not move, compensation would not fit, or insufficient strength in important parts of the job. Some of these telephone conversations will lead to a decision to meet for a more detailed discussion and interview. Before the search is completed, the consultant will usually have been in contact with a large number, sometimes well over 300 people. He must record all of these conversations and ensure that everyone is eventually thanked and informed of the disposition of their participation. All of these communications must be accomplished without revealing the identity of the client, except in those specific situations in which the client gives permission to do so.

Throughout these steps, you and your consultant will have been in regular contact. You will be well aware of his progress and will have responded to his discussions with you of "sample" executives. It sometimes happens that one more of these samples sounds so good that you may ask the consultant to identify him and immediately present him as a candidate. The consultant must first determine whether the "sample" wants to be a candidate or is at least willing to have his identity revealed and to explore the opportunity. In addition, the consultant will usually have to update data on his position, his compensation, his performance, and his reputation. The resulting information, or the "sample" himself, may cause a conclusion that he is not a candidate.

In researching the files, your consultant may discover an apparent "gem"—an executive who appears to be ideal for the vacant position. This situation poses an interesting question. Should the "gem" immediately be recommended to you by your consultant or should the consultant wait until he is far enough into the search to be absolutely certain that the "gem" should be among the best candidates who can be found? If you have the right partnership relationship with your consultant, he will feel free to tell you about the "gem" without delay, and then both of you can decide whether you should interview him immediately or wait until the search is further along.

Recently, an executive search firm undertook an assignment to find a Chief Financial Officer for a Chicago-based corporation. During the same week that the search commenced, the consultant was contacted by the Corporate Vice President Finance of another Chicago corporation that had just been acquired. The executive was being asked to move to New York to be a backup for the 63-year-old Chief Financial Officer of the parent company. He did not want to leave Chicago. He had all of the professional, executive, and personality qualifications for the consultant's client assignment. A decision would have to be made quickly because the executive could not keep the parent company waiting.

In this case, the consultant, after arranging with the executive to make some discrete checks on him, discussed the prospective candidate with his client who immediately expressed strong interest. However, it then became apparent that it would be impossible within the available time frame for all of the senior people in the client company with whom the executive would have to work closely to spend enough time with the prospective candidate to be confident that he was the most likely, among anyone who could be recruited, to succeed as their new Chief Financial Officer. When the time and scheduling problems could not be properly resolved, the consultant advised his client against taking a shortcut by yielding to the temptation to hire this immediately available "gem." Both client and consultant came to the conclusion, reluctantly, that it would be wiser to forego this apparently golden opportunity rather than make the important decision to hire the "gem" without everyone concerned having had adequate opportunity to evaluate him.

There is a difference of opinion among executive search consultants on the number of executives who should be reviewed with a client during the course of a search. Some consultants are inclined toward the idea that, as professionals, they should not discuss their work with their clients but should simply present one or two or perhaps even three candidates when their search is completed and then help the client to recruit the selected candidate. These consultants are of the opinion that they are paid to do the job and that they should not involve clients any more than is absolutely necessary. They also cite the importance of confidentiality and of protecting the information given to them by sources, references, and prospective candidates.

At the other end of the spectrum are consultants who keep their clients informed on the details of the entire search. They list all of the executives who have been considered and those who have been contacted. They explain why some have been rejected and why others have decided not to explore the opportunity. They review with their clients all of the companies whose executives have been researched. Some consultants compile all of this information into a written report on the search. They strive to be able to answer any question that their clients may ask about any executive whose position might qualify him as a prospective candidate.

Who among these consultants is right?

Here again, the answer lies in partnership between consultant and client. As a client, you have the right to be kept as fully informed as necessary to give you the assurance that a thorough professional job is being done for you. On the other hand, your consultant's integrity would certainly be suspect if he were to reveal information on contacts that he has had with prospective candidates, without obtaining their permission to do so. Some executives, at least initially, refuse to allow their names to be revealed to a client unless the client is identified to them first.

If you have selected a highly reputable search firm, if you have confidence in your consultant and have established with him a thorough understanding on how you will work together, then the two of you will be able to find a path, for each search, that will usually take you between these two extremes of the spectrum but might, at times, follow one of the extremes.

For example, a conglomerate with headquarters in New York decided to replace the President of one of its industrial products divisions. There were almost two hundred companies in the same industry as this division. The headquarters executives were familiar with many of the Presidents of these companies. The agreement between client and consultant in this case required the consultant to evaluate the Presidents of a selected group of companies and, in addition, to extend the search to the second level of several large competitors. The consultant proposed that he should also ensure that senior executives who may have moved to other industries should be included in the search. The search firm's research department enabled the consultant to eliminate many names from the list because the information on them did not fit the desired profile. Those that were contacted either eliminated themselves, were rejected by the consultant, or were asked for permission to discuss them confidentially with the client. Mainly because of the excellent reputation of the search firm and the professional behavior of the consultant, there was not a single refusal to grant permission to reveal the identity of a prospective candidate—and this was accomplished without identifying the client. The search was successfully completed.

On the other hand, in another case involving a highly confidential search for a CEO of a substantial corporation, the search consultant insisted that he must be able to talk to other CEOs in the same and related industries without any obligation to report the results to his client. The consultant was of the opinion that unless he could give his prospective candidates an ironclad guarantee of secrecy upon his first contact with them, he could not succeed. The client, in this case, agreed. The only progress that was regularly reported to the client was the estimated percentage of prospective candidates that had been contacted and evaluated so far. Two names were finally recommended to the client, together with complete dossiers. Both candidates, of course, had given their permission to be identified. This search was also successfully completed.

A problem that is sometimes encountered by search firms is a decision by the client, during the search, to change the specifications. The cause of the change can often be traced back to failure by the client and the consultant to have thoroughly analyzed the objectives and goals of the position and the qualifications required to achieve them. In some cases, the cause of the change is mainly one of seeing the position from a different perspective as a result of discussing several executives with the consultant and of interviewing two or three prospective candidates. Their involvement in the search project is often the first time that senior level executives of the client organization have acquired a detailed knowledge of the backgrounds, experience, opinions, and thinking processes of executives from other companies who are in positions similar to the one to be filled. The input from these discussions and interviews can stimulate a review of the position and even the organization's structure, which in turn can produce a decision to make changes. The changes sometimes result in cancelling the search because the conclusion is reached that the position can be combined with another one, or that the incumbent should be retained in the position, or that another executive within the company should be promoted into the open position.

In a recent case, a search firm in the U.S.A. was retained by a European company to fill the President and Chief Operating Officer (COO) position of its U.S. subsidiary. The Chairman and Chief Executive Officer of the subsidiary had been sent to the U.S. several years ago from the parent organization. Four candidates were interviewed by the U.S. CEO but also by several senior executives from the parent company in Europe. The interviews gave the parent company executives quite a different perspective of the U.S. and of their U.S. Chairman. They decided to cancel that search and start another one to bring in a new Chairman and CEO.

A mistake that is sometimes made by organizations that retain search firms is to demand that a large number of candidates be presented for interviews. Some think that only in this way will they receive full value. Others seem to enjoy interviewing numerous executives for a position. This is a mistake that can cause the consultant to lower his standards and to substitute quantity for quality. It should be the consultant's function and not the client's to interview a large number of candidates. Otherwise, the client is encouraging the consultant to behave like an employment agency. An important part of the consultant's role is to exercise his professional judgment so that the candidates who are interviewed by his client have been so thoroughly evaluated that any one of them would represent the best that could be presented. The only reason for presenting more than one is because it is usually impossible for the consultant to precisely predict the human chemistry between the candidate and the several executives in the client organization who will interview him.

Returning to the example that was introduced earlier in this chapter, the search for the Chief Financial Officer will have followed all of the search steps including the research, "sourcing," contacting, screening, checking, discussing, and interviewing by the consultant until both client and consultant are satisfied that the two or three or possibly four best candidates have been found. During the course of the search, the consultant, sometimes assisted by his researchers, will have talked with over one hundred or perhaps several hundred executives. Had the search been multicountry, the consultants in the search firm's offices abroad would have followed the same steps, directed by the consultant in charge of the project. In some such cases, the client will have asked him to interview all of the potential candidates, no matter where they are.

In the next chapter, assessing executives will be discussed, and in Chapter Nine, the presentation, interviewing, and selection of candidates will be described.

Chapter Eight

The Art and Science of Assessing Candidates

There are many stories about famous entrepreneurs who have met executives for the first time by chance and hired them on the spot. At the other end of the spectrum are organizations that, in addition to multiple and repeat interviews by several of their executives, put every candidate through a one-day or two-day psychological assessment process. Many European companies will not make executive hiring decisions until their graphologist has given his opinion based upon analysis of the candidate's handwriting. Which of these procedures is right or wrong, better or worse?

There is more art than science in the assessing of executives. Every organization develops methods either haphazardly or systematically, that seem to suit them. There is constant controversy in every organization on this subject because it is so difficult to measure results.

When assessing an executive candidate, we are trying to predict his behavior and his performance in a situation and an environment that is new and different to him. The methods that are available for measuring the situation and environment are neither precise nor is there a common denominator. This means that we are forced to rely on the judgments of those who are describing the organization and the vacant position to establish the criteria that will be used as a measure for predicting the candidate's behavior and performance. This is why the importance of this descriptive step is so strongly emphasized in Chapter Six. This is part of the reason why every organization differs in their efforts to assess executives.

The other reason for the variations in methods of assessment is the differences of opinion over the effectiveness of the tools that are used in the assessment process. Despite the publicity given to those famous cases of hiring on the spot, it would be difficult to find a responsible CEO who would recommend this procedure to his organization.

The main means of assessing executives are:

Interviews

Background investigations

Informal socializing

Psychological assessments

Those who utilize psychological assessments to assist in predicting executive behavior and performance point out that the experienced industrial psychologist brings to the problem a body of specialized knowledge that greatly increases the chances of making the best decisions and reduces the risk of making a serious mistake. They reason that it would be inadvisable to try to solve complex legal, medical, accounting, and engineering problems without the advice of lawyers, doctors, accountants, and engineers. Why then, they ask, would anyone make a vital decision on executive placement without the advice of a psychologist? Their list of justifications includes their views that most executives are poor interviewers, that they tend to select people with whom they have common tastes, interests, and backgrounds, and with whom they feel comfortable, rather than those who are best qualified. They explain that the psychologist's in-depth analysis of the successful candidate enables his superiors to better understand how to work with him effectively.

Some of the most thorough psychological assessment work is done by teams of three psychologists. One does the in-depth interviewing. Another administers the tests. Each prepares a separate report and submits it to the third psychologist who is the supervisor. Any significant disagreement between the two reports must be resolved or explained.

The organizations that have chosen not to utilize psychological assessments build their case on a number of arguments. First and foremost is the problem of describing the situation and environment against which the executive is to be assessed, in measurable terms. In the absence of measurable criteria, they say, the psychologists' judgment is too subjective. Another is the questionable validity of the tests. A third is the probability that the psychologist, rather than the responsible executives, will make the selection decision because no one would dare hire against the psychologist's advice. A fourth is the concern over the likelihood that truly outstanding candidates would be eliminated because of personality problems. A fifth is the belief that some good candidates would refuse to be assessed while others learn how to manipulate the tests and the assessment interviews. In addition, some organizations that have international operations doubt that it is possible to overcome the influence on assessment results of different culture systems. Finally, there is the concern about the extra time that an employed candidate must find for the assessment, in addition to all of the interviews.

The effects of differences in culture systems were quite evident when a multinational corporation attempted to validate its U.S. psychological assessment package in Europe. One of the standard questions asked by the American psychologists was, "In what position do you expect to be ten years from now?" Most of the sample group of European executives replied that this would be entirely up to the top management of their company. Most U.S. executives would have replied very differently, leaving no doubt that in ten years they would expect to have achieved a substantially larger responsibility.

Executive search firms do not normally use psychological assessments. For them, there is the practical consideration of candidate willingness, time, and cost, keeping in mind that most of a search firm's candidates are not seeking another position but have been sought after. Furthermore, client organizations that have their own psychological assessment arrangements would usually be unwilling to accept an outsider's report. In such cases, the candidates might well have to be asked to undergo a second assessment. Finally, executive search firms are mostly of the opinion that their professional consultants are so skilled in judging the suitability of an executive through interviews and other sources of information that they do not need psychological assessment reports on their candidates.

There are situations, however, in which a search consultant may recommend a psychological evaluation of a candidate. A case in point involved a search for a Director of Marketing for the international pharmaceutical division of a health care company. Some members of top management favored an internal candidate while the Vice President

International and some other key people were strongly in favor of recruiting from outside. Of the three candidates presented by the search firm, one was strongly favored by the Vice President International and those who supported him in his outside recruitment efforts. Those who favored the internal candidate insisted that the outsider's personality would not fit. They cited his tendency to be wordy, to exaggerate, and to name-drop and felt that his aggressiveness would irritate everyone. On the other hand, the candidate had an excellent record, with no indication of significant interpersonal-relationship problems.

The search consultant suggested that a psychological assessment, with particular emphasis on the alleged personality problems, might help to settle the argument. Agreement was reached among all concerned and great care was taken in selecting the psychologist. The candidate was persuaded to cooperate, and the suggestion was implemented. The resulting report helped those who were against the candidate to understand that the aggressiveness was an important factor in the executive's impressive record and that he could bring refreshing and effective changes to the company. The outsider was hired.

If your organization makes a practice of psychological assessment of all executive candidates, this should be clearly spelled out to the consultant before the search begins. The consultant can then inform candidates in advance. It is also advisable for you to introduce the psychologist who is responsible for your assessments to your consultant so that the consultant is conversant with the procedures that candidates will follow, and the psychologist can discuss the criteria that will be used in assessing the candidates.

At the point at which your search consultant recommends a candidate to you, he will at least have discretely obtained opinions from two or more people who have worked with the candidate, and he will have thoroughly interviewed him. During the interview, the consultant will have obtained information on the executive's current and past positions and general background. The following list is an example of the data that should have been obtained by your consultant.

Personal

Surname

Christian names

Nickname

Birthdate

Birthplace

Where raised

Citizenship

Migratory status

Does executive have physical handicaps?

Health problems?

When was his last complete physical examination?

Has he undergone psychological assessment? Can report be made available?

Marital

Married

Single

Divorced

Widowed

Separated

Previous marriages

Children's ages and sexes

Spouse's first and (if applicable) maiden name
Birthplace
Citizenship
Education
Languages
Work? If so, give details

Education

Universities attended
Periods attended

Majors

Degrees

Languages

What languages does he speak?

How well?

Experience

Information required about present and each previous employer

Name of company or organization

Sales volume

Number of people

Main product lines or services

Location of headquarters

Parent company

Location of headquarters of parent company

Date executive started with company

Date that he left company

Was his compensation extended beyond termination date?

If so, for how long?

What were reasons for leaving company?

For every position held with every employer beginning with present position

Position title

Location

From when to when (month/year)

To whom did he report?
Name
Title
Location

To whom did his superior report?
Name
Title
Location

For how many people was he responsible?

For what products or services was he responsible?

For what sales volume was he responsible?

Compensation

Base salary

Bonus formula

Latest bonus amount

Deferred compensation formula

Deferred compensation amount

Other incentive compensation

Company contribution to savings plan or other plans

Other forms of cash compensation

Gross cash compensation

Foreign service allowances (if based abroad)

Tax equalization (if based abroad)

Estimated net after-tax income from company compensation

Company benefits
Life insurance
Accident insurance
Medical insurance
Pension plan

Other benefits

Stock options

Stock plans

Company automobile

Chauffeur

Company-paid club membership

Home leave (if based abroad)

Other forms of direct or indirect compensation or benefits

Other perquisites

Date of last salary increase and amount

Date of next expected salary increase and amount

Estimated amounts that would be sacrificed from bonus, deferred compensation, pension plan, stock options, and any other forms of compensation, if executive joins another organization

Estimated total compensation package that would be required to attract this executive to position for which he is being considered

Miscellaneous

Would he and his family be willing to relocate?
Nationally?
Internationally?

Are there locations that he would refuse?

What are his preferred locations?

How much business travel would be acceptable?

References

Of whom may we ask a number of questions regarding his performance and behavior in his present and previous organizations?

Supplementary information

There should be several additional pages of notes on organization structures and relationships, functions, responsibilities, authorities, accountabilities, results achieved, and circumstances for every significant position. For example, what were the actual circumstances of the dramatic improvement in sales and profits? Was it mainly due to new products that had already been planned or was it largely the result of the prospective candidate's effectiveness? The consultant must be especially perceptive and knowledgable in judging responses to these questions when the prospective candidate is with a matrix organization.

All of this information, together with the consultant's opinions, should be summarized and presented to you in written form. Each search firm has its own format for this purpose. Executives who retain search firms have their preferences on documentation presented by the consultant. Therefore, formats can vary from a brief résumé accompanied by verbal discussion, to a multipage letter or a multisection dossier. These presentation documents are discussed more fully in Chapter Nine.

Should the spouse and the candidate's family life be assessed? If so, to what extent? Some executives believe that their wives and families and their marital situation are all part of their private lives and should not even be discussed with a potential employer. Unless such people are exceptionally or uniquely qualified for the position, they should not be given further consideration. Why? Because spouse and family life can change an otherwise effective, dedicated executive into a neurotic disaster. A spouse who resents the change, who cannot adapt, who is indiscrete, or without the needed social graces can cause serious problems. The willingness of an executive to consider a move to another company is sometimes influenced by an unhappy marriage or an extramarital affair from which he wants to escape. In all cases, but especially when the vacant position involves leadership of a large group or requires residing in a smaller community or basing in a foreign country, it is essential that enough is known about the candidate's marital and family situation and history to be confident that they will be assets rather than liabilities.

At the point at which you and your colleagues begin to interview a candidate, you will already have substantial information about him from your consultant. Your task now is to decide whether the executive is the best that you are likely to find for your requirements.

Your first step is to satisfy yourself that the candidate meets all of the criteria that have been listed as essentials. Next comes an evaluation of the desired or preferred but not essential qualifications. Then should come a thorough questioning of all aspects of the candidate's positions until you are convinced that there are no serious defects in his experience. The following checklist, used by an executive search firm, may help you during the interview to probe all of the factors that would help you to judge the candidate's suitability.

A. *Effectiveness*

1. How well does the candidate manage his time?

2. How well does the candidate choose what he should contribute to the organization to produce the best results?

3. How well does the candidate mobilize his own strengths and those of others to achieve desired goals?

4. How well does the candidate select priorities and adhere to them?

5. How well does the candidate choose which decisions to make?

6. Does the candidate's decision making give sufficient weight to deciding what should not be done?

7. How effective are the candidate's decisions and his follow-through?

B. *Abilities*

1. Entrepreneurial capability

2. Analytical ability

3. Problem-solving ability

4. Planning capability

5. Negotiating ability

6. Team building and management capability

7. Turnaround abilities

8. Start-up abilities

9. Leadership abilities

10. How articulate is the candidate?

11. Is the candidate skilled at making presentations?

12. Is the candidate a follower rather than a leader?

13. Is the candidate a team player?

14. Is the candidate an individual contributor rather than a manager?

15. Is the candidate primarily a staff rather than a line executive?

16. How good is the candidate's judgment?

17. Potential for next 2 levels

C. *Impression*

1. Appropriateness of cultural background

2. Appearance

3. How well does the candidate dress?

4. Grooming

5. Charisma

6. Overall personality

7. Overweight?

8. Table manners

9. Social graces

10. How well does the candidate handle himself in an interview?

D. *Track record*

1. General management track record

2. Marketing management track record

3. Sales management track record

4. Technology management track record

5. Human resources management track record

6. Technical services management track record

7. Financial management track record

8. Manufacturing management track record

9. Experience in client's markets

10. Experience with client's type of product

11. Merger, acquisition, joint venture, licensing experience

12. Growth results record

13. Profit results record

14. Share of market record

15. Recruiting experience

16. Track record in planning, training, and development of his organization and people, short and long range

17. Track record in short and long range business planning and implementation

18. The candidate's compensation pattern track record

E. *Adequacy of education*

1. Human resources education

2. Executive education

3. Professional education

4. Required/desired languages

F. *Interpersonal*

1. Interpersonal skills–superiors

2. Interpersonal skills–peers

3. Interpersonal skills–subordinates

4. Interpersonal skills–markets

5. Interpersonal skills–public

G. *Habits*

1. Work habits

2. Leisure habits

3. How well does the candidate take care of himself?

4. Drinking habits

5. Does the candidate smoke?

6. Drug usage/addiction

H. *Characteristics and behavior*

1. Integrity/honesty

2. Self-confidence

3. Drive

4. Initiative

5. Creativity

6. Maturity level

7. Maze brightness

8. Intelligence

9. Adaptability

10. Toughness

11. Stability

12. Reliability

13. Appropriateness of temperament

14. Sense of humor

15. Is the candidate arrogant, pompous?

16. How does the candidate behave/perform under heavy stress?

17. Does the candidate handle problems logically rather than emotionally?

18. Does the candidate give top priority to the company's interests rather than his own?

Until now, you have been asking questions and sensing carefully with ears, eyes, and antenna. The next step is to describe to the candidate the organization, its executives, and the vacant position as realistically as possible, including the negatives as well as the positives. The description should be accompanied by examples of incidents, situations, and problems. The candidate will have been given all or most of this information by the consultant, but it is essential to complete understanding that he also hears it from you, and for you to observe his responses. In addition to the personality and behavior of your organization and its executives, the structure and operating policies should be carefully reviewed. Such important subjects as matrix and centralization versus decentralization need to be fully covered. There should be ample opportunity for the candidate to ask questions, to comment, and to respond. The purposes of this exercise are to enable the candidate to decide whether he really wants the position, and for you to ensure that there will be no reason, if the candidate is hired, for him to claim later that he did not understand what he was getting into.

An extreme case in point was an assignment undertaken several years ago for General Somoza by an international executive search firm. Having had a heart attack and becoming more involved with combatting the growing revolution in his country, the General requested the search firm to help him to recruit a top-level executive who could take over responsibility for his business interests. When the search was completed, the General was especially intrigued with one candidate but kept expressing to the consultant his concern as to whether the candidate would have the guts to stand by Somoza if the revolution became worse. Finally, arrangements were made for the candidate to spend several days with Somoza in his bunker in Nicaragua, from where the battle was being directed. During those few days, there was an earthquake at 3 A.M. through which the candidate slept peacefully and a bazooka attack on the bunker from a hotel room two floors below the candidate's room. Finally, the candidate had to be accompanied to the airport by armed guards. When the candidate continued to express strong interest in the position, Somoza was satisfied that the candidate had been sufficiently exposed to the realities of the position.

Having ensured that the candidate thoroughly understands the functions, objectives, goals, authorities, responsibilities, accountabilities and relationships, the informal as well as the formal organization, and the personalities of the executives and of the organization, the next step is to consciously review your own biases by asking yourself whether your reactions to and judgments of the candidate are entirely objective. Experienced search consultants can tell you that the senior executives of some companies will immediately reject anyone whose appearance or background does not fit their mold, no matter how well qualified. Other senior executives are especially impressed by loquacious candidates and refuse to be convinced that other factors should be given greater weight. Fluency in foreign languages and complete biculturalism often cause organizations to hire second and third rate executives for their international operations simply because they feel more comfortable with them than with an obvious foreigner with a strong accent who is far more competent.

Several years ago, a major U.S. multinational company in the consumer products field was suffering severe losses in Mexico. They decided to replace their American Managing Director with two executives. One was to be a Mexican whose sole job as Chairman would be to establish and maintain better relations with the government. The other was to be an American General Manager who would be instructed to turn the company around by enlarging it and capturing a greater percentage of the market. They were about to hire the Mexican when they asked an international search firm to help them to recruit the General Manager.

The Mexican candidate for the Chairman position whom they had found themselves, and by whom they were overwhelmed, was socially prominent, wealthy, U.S. educated, bicultural, bilingual, with excellent high-level contacts, but no real business track record. The consultant strongly advised his client to scrap the whole idea and instead to hire only one executive for both jobs—a hard-nosed Mexican with a good turnaround record and proven ability to negotiate effectively with the government. Mainly because the losses were multiplying to staggering proportions, the headquarters eventually agreed to hire a candidate who matched the tough specifications recommended by the consultant. Several months after joining them, the new Mexican CEO advised them to

shut down and liquidate their entire operation and to reach an agreement with the government to reinvest the proceeds in Mexico. They
agreed. Subsequent events proved that had the headquarters people
exercised their biases, the losses could have been astronomical.

A candidate will often behave quite differently in a social situation
than he does in an interview. Your consultant will probably have taken
him to lunch or dinner as a step in assessing his personality and predicting his behavior. His wife may have been included. Certainly, your
consultant should insist that you and other executives in the company
who would be working closely with him should socialize with him and
his wife. Not only do such events provide another opportunity to understand the candidate's personality and his family life, but they help to
ensure that your organization will not be seriously embarrassed in the
future by the social behavior of the candidate or his wife.

An essential step in the assessment process that is often handled
superficially by organizations is incorrectly labelled as "reference checking." What is really needed is a background investigation. Its main
purpose is to enable you and the consultant to see and understand the
candidate through the perceptions of people who have worked closely
with him. Another purpose, of course, is to make certain that the candidate is telling the truth about his experience.

The candidate, in most cases, is not seeking another position. The
consultant's discussions with him on your behalf and your meetings
with him must be conducted in strictest confidence. These circumstances make it difficult to determine when and how to conduct the
background investigation. In most cases, an experienced consultant can
convince the candidate that it is in his interest as well as that of his
client to cooperate in the confidential background investigation. Usually, with the help and permission of the candidate, executives can be
identified who have previously held positions in the same organization
as the candidate, close enough to him to have a thorough knowledge of
his behavior, performance, and reputation. Ideally, one or more of these
executives will have been the candidate's immediate superior.

Your consultant will have asked for a guarantee of confidentiality
from each reference and will make it clear that the candidate is not
seeking another position, but has been approached by the consultant.
He will then question the reference very thoroughly, using his candi-
date-interview check list and data as a guide. The consultant will carefully explain all aspects of the position for which the candidate is being
considered. Finally, he will seek the reference's opinion of the candi-

date's suitability and will usually end by asking, Would you hire him for this position?

There are, of course, organizations that specialize in investigating educational records, police records, credit, and other aspects of an executive's private life. Your consultant will only have utilized such services at the executive level in rare cases in which he suspects that the candidate may be trying to mislead him. As integrity is an absolutely essential quality in a candidate, any doubts that the consultant has about his truthfulness will probably have resulted in the candidate's rejection without the use of such specialized services.

The interviews and the background investigation should be so thorough that there is no doubt in the consultant's mind about the candidate's suitability. It is the consultant's responsibility to ensure that you and your organization will not subsequently discover anything significantly negative about the candidate.

As a final step in the assessment process, it is always wise for you and your consultant to take the trouble to review once again the position description and specification and compare it with your assessment of the candidate. By doing so, you will decrease the chances of your assessment being too heavily influenced by biases that could lead to a serious mistake.

On the other hand, in going through these assessment steps, there are always two important questions that are, at times, the most difficult to answer. One of these questions concerns your own judgment of the human chemistry. Will you and your organization, in the final analysis, be able to interact with this candidate so that the results, short- and long-range, will achieve your objectives? The other question applies to the unusual, the especially talented candidate who does not fit the specifications entirely. Should you sacrifice a requirement of the position in exchange for that unique talent? If you have chosen a highly effective executive search consultant, and if you and he have established the recommended close working partnership for this project, your consultant's counsel should be invaluable to you in helping you to answer these questions.

In the next chapter, the interviewing and selection steps will be discussed.

Chapter Nine

Working with Your Executive Search Firm During the Interviewing and Selection of Candidates

A major cause of the loss of outstanding candidates is delay. From the moment that he expresses a willingness to explore the opportunity with your organization, a good executive will usually be asking himself and probably others, "Would this be the wisest move for me at this stage of my career?" Although your consultant will have advised the candidate against revealing to his employers that he has been approached by an executive search firm, he will undoubtedly be at least subtly sounding out those within his organization who can help him to evaluate his future. He may also seek the advice of his close business acquaintances and friends outside his organization on the pros and cons of making the suggested move. These conversations often lead to the sudden surfacing of other opportunities within and outside his organization. The risk of losing the candidate to one of these other situations increases dramatically with the passage of time between the first contact with him by your consultant and the firm offer of employment from your company.

When an outstanding candidate is lost, the entire search project is usually adversely affected. Although one or two other candidates will probably have been presented to you, it often happens that other candidates do not quite seem to measure up to the lost one, especially if he is the one whom you have selected, and the search has to be reactivated in an effort to develop an equally outstanding prospect. Therefore, it is essential that you and your organization and the consultant give high priority to expediting the process of interviewing and selecting the candidate.

In fact, all of the good work done so far can be totally undone if the interviewing and selection process overall is not well managed. You have reached a point at which numerous man-hours have been spent and funds invested to enable you and your colleagues to begin interviewing the two or three or possibly four candidates that have been developed as a result of all of the steps that have been described in previous chapters. Surely common sense indicates that sufficient time and attention must be applied to ensure that everything within reason is done to maximize the chances now of making the best possible selection and to avoid losing a good candidate. Unfortunately, it is at this stage that many executive search assignments fail.

The close working partnership between you and your consultant continues to be essential. Ease and frequency of communication between you are absolutely necessary.

Before a candidate is interviewed, the consultant will have supplied the decriptive documentation that has been agreed upon. As discussed in Chapter Eight, this documentation can take many different forms, but it will provide the information that is needed (1) to ensure that the candidate meets the specifications and (2) to provide the information required to enable you to conduct your interviews effectively.

As a result of the discussions with your consultant and the information that he has presented in written form, a decision will have been made to commence interviewing. This part of the entire project requires the same careful management and attention to detail as does every other part. The three objectives now are to assess the candidates, to select one for the vacant position, and to make a positive impression on all two or three of them from the beginning to the end of the process.

As a professional, the consultant will have commenced, from his first contact with the candidate, to develop a positive image of your organization. Everything that he and you and your colleagues do with the candidates from then on will either continue to build on that image or damage or destroy it. As an overall guide to handling this phase of the project, it would be well for you and your colleagues to ask yourselves how you would like to be treated under all of the circumstances in which the candidate will find himself.

One of the first mistakes to avoid is to treat the candidate as if he is an applicant—someone who is trying to find another job. Even if this is the case, he should not be considered unless he is outstanding, and this means that you still must compete for him. More often, the candidate has not been thinking of leaving his present employer and has been persuaded by your consultant that your organization can offer him a better position and that he should explore it.

When scheduling the first and any subsequent interviews, you and your colleagues should be flexible and considerate. The candidate cannot usually absent himself from his current work with no plausible explanation, and he does not want to have to lie to his superiors in order to excuse himself for the interview. This means that interview arrangements should be made that are convenient to the candidate and once arranged, they should not be changed by you. If he is based in another city or country, it may be necessary to meet him on a weekend. If in the same city, interviews should be arranged outside normal working hours if necessary. For the first interview, you or one of your colleagues might meet the candidate somewhere close to his present base. If the results of that first meeting are positive, arrangements for getting together with your other colleagues can then be made.

A good example is the case of a company on the West Coast that was seeking a Vice President Research and Development. Their executive search consultant had succeeded in interesting an excellent executive for the position who was based in New Jersey. The consultant had already had two after-hours meetings with the candidate alone and a third at dinner that included the candidate's wife. As a next step, the Vice President Personnel made a special trip to New Jersey to interview the candidate. The meeting was arranged in a nearby hotel suite in the early evening and included dinner. The discussions went so well that the candidate invited the Vice President Personnel to his home after dinner to meet his wife and family.

However, the candidate, although positively impressed by the West Coast company, was reluctant to take the risk of changing employers. He had been with his company for 14 years, had been promoted several times, and was highly regarded. He and his family were active in the community, and the three children were doing well in their schools. Both the consultant and the Vice President Personnel were of the opinion that, for many reasons, the open position would be the right move for the candidate at that stage of his career and that he was the best qualified executive who could be found for the position. They both informed the President accordingly. The President then made a special trip to New Jersey for a weekend meeting with the candidate during which he reached the same conclusion as had the consultant and the Vice President Personnel. The candidate was so positively impressed that he accepted the President's invitation to make a weekend visit to the West Coast headquarters and to meet the other executives with whom he would be working. During that weekend, he spent time with them and the President in their offices and three of their homes, including the President's home. The candidate became convinced that he should respond positively to their proposal to join their firm. The consultant suggested, and it was agreed, that his wife should participate in the decision. Another weekend trip was quickly arranged that included the candidate's wife to enable both to visit the residential areas and for her to meet the executives with whom her husband would be working, and their wives. The outcome was positive and the candidate was hired.

Throughout the entire effort, the candidate was given V.I.P. treatment. He was treated with the utmost consideration while at the same being thoroughly evaluated and fully informed of the negatives as well as the positives of the company and the open position. Particular attention was given to answering his questions. There were no delays and no changes in the meeting and visiting arrangements. Five weeks elapsed between the first contact and acceptance of the offer.

By contrast, the following case is described because it includes almost all of the mistakes that could be made in conducting an executive search. Every aspect was so badly handled that it sounds like fiction, but it is a true story.

In this case, both the Chairman and the President of a privately held, medium-sized, multinational company decided that they would retire within two years. They concluded that there was no executive within the company who could qualify as Chief Executive Officer (CEO) within that period, especially as the performance of the company had been declining for some time. They decided to recruit a CEO from outside the company. They chose to use but outsmart executive search firms and to devise their own means of ensuring that their decision to recruit the CEO from outside would not be revealed to anyone else in their company.

Their first step was to fire a Vice President who headed one of their sicker divisions. Next, they gradually engaged the services of several executive search firms to replace the Vice President. They did not tell these firms that any other search firm was working on the same assignment. The specifications given to the search firms were for the Vice

President rather than the CEO. Concurrently, they placed camouflaged advertisements for the position in major newspapers. After each search firm had been working on the assignment just long enough to present candidates, they terminated the firms' services. Their reasoning was that through this strategy they would get the broadest possible exposure to prospective candidates and that among the executives who would be presented to them for the Vice President position, they would find a candidate for the CEO position. In the meantime, no one would be aware of their real objective.

For over a year, both the Chairman and the President devoted a substantial percentage of their time to screening the hundreds of responses to their ads, reviewing recommendations from the search firms, and discussing and interviewing prospective candidates. Despite the pleadings of the consultants, the two executives treated candidates as if they were job applicants in the factory. Interview schedules were frequently changed. Candidates were kept waiting for an hour or more. Initial interviews generally lasted only 30 minutes and those candidates who "passed" during the first interview were asked to return. Many candidates rejected the second invitation despite the best efforts of the consultants. The Chairman and President refused to be guided by the consultants. For example, their first question to candidates who had been presented by the consultants to explore the opportunity was, Why are you looking for a job? In the meantime, the performance of the company continued to decline. As none of the search firms were seeking candidates who were qualified for the top job and as any outstanding candidate was turned off by the way in which interviews were handled, the whole project was an expensive failure. More than two years from the start of the effort, having learned a lesson, they succeeded in recruiting the new CEO by engaging the services of yet another search firm, giving the firm the right specifications and following the consultant's advice on handling the interviews and selection.

In a third case, the organization is a worldwide engineering company whose growth rate has exceeded its ability to develop executives fast enough to meet their requirements. Their remarkable success is due to the excellence of their top management. Every year they recruit a number of executives from all over the world. They have a matrix structure. Their Vice President Personnel has the staff responsibility for executive recruitment. Some of the requirements are handled directly by him and his staff, while others are assigned by him to one of three approved executive search firms. For each executive recruitment assignment, the

Vice President Personnel organizes a project team comprised of the line and staff executives who are either responsible for or directly associated with the open position and who will, therefore, participate in the hiring decision. The CEO has made it very clear that top priority must be given by their project teams to every executive search assignment.

The project teams participate in the development of the position description and specification. They interview all of the candidates recommended by the Vice President Personnel. They make the selection recommendation. Most of the candidates have to be brought from distant locations. The Vice President Personnel and his staff as well as the selected executive search consultants are so knowledgeable of the company and its standards that they are able to thoroughly prescreen a candidate before he is brought to headquarters to be interviewed by the project teams. The spouse is usually also invited. During the candidate's visit to the headquarters, the interviews are well organized. Enough time is devoted to thoroughly assess the candidate and to answer all of his questions. The interview trips of the two or three candidates for each position are arranged with minimum delay so that the lapse of time between the first contact and the hiring decision is minimized. Candidates are promptly informed whether an offer will be forthcoming. Under these circumstances, most candidates are asked to make only one visit to the headquarters. The successful candidate usually makes a second visit for the negotiations. The company has been remarkably successful in attracting outstanding executives.

Two questions that are frequently asked about the interviewing and selecting process are (1) Are group interviews more effective than one to one interviews? (2) Should the consultant be present during the interviews?

To the first question, the answer is that both one to one and group interviews can be used effectively. Most organizations always use one to one interviews to obtain all of the information needed and to make the initial evaluation. Those that also arrange group interviews organize them carefully so that the candidate is not given a negative impression. The group interviews are generally used as a final step in the assessment process.

The answer to the second question is generally yes. By observing the interviews, the consultant can gain a far better understanding of the reasons for his client's preference for one candidate over another or for rejection of his candidates. As many executives handle candidate interviews badly, the consultant can be much more effective in providing guidance on interviewing when needed. When the selection decision is being made, his advice is often more useful and credible if he has observed the interviews.

Most executives have had no training and only sporadic experience in interviewing. They are often poor listeners. Listening is a skill that needs to be learned and constantly practiced. Too often, the executive who is conducting the interview does most of the talking, and when the candidate is responding, the executive is frequently thinking about what he is going to ask or say next instead of concentrating on what the candidate is transmitting by his words and overall behavior. Your consultant can help to ensure that you and your colleagues are not guilty of these undesirable practices.

When all of the interviews have been completed, many firms use an evaluation form for the selection process. The form is comprised of several basic questions that are keyed to the position description and specifications. Usually an overall rating or grading is requested. These forms are filled out for each candidate by everyone who interviewed them. The project team leader, who is frequently the Vice President Personnel or a member of his staff, then summarizes the responses from the forms. With this information, the project team usually meets or communicates by phone to reach a conclusion. In most organizations, the final selection decision is made by the executive directly and immediately responsible for the open position and by that executive's superior.

The final selection of the candidate is a vital decision that will have a direct effect upon the performance of the organization. Usually, the decision develops gradually, as candidates are interviewed and discussed. When it is made, the next step is to inform the candidate without delay. The manner and circumstances in which he is advised of the decision are important. Consideration needs to be given to such questions as: Who will talk to him? Should it be done in person or by phone? Should the conversation include the terms of the offer or should terms be discussed subsequently? The answers to these questions will vary with circumstances. When the interviewing and selection process is handled effectively, the stage is set for the next important step—the negotiations.

Chapter Ten

Negotiations
Between Organization
and Candidate

A conglomerate had acquired a company in an industry with great growth potential. The President of the company became the President of the new division. Twelve months later, the parent company decided to replace the Division President because of failure to achieve the targets of the business plan. An executive search firm was retained to fill the vacant position. The specifications required an executive with a strong track record in the same industry but with a style and personality that would fit the parent.

The search covered every company in the industry. One executive stood out as being by far the best qualified. He was the President of a smaller but highly successful company. At first, he was reluctant to consider a move, not only because of his satisfaction with his present company but also due to his family situation. Nevertheless, over a period of weeks he became gradually more interested in the opportunities offered by the new position. He was interviewed by several of the conglomerate executives in strict secrecy. Finally, he told the search consultant that he would consider an offer.

He had, as usual, a complex compensation package that included stock options, deferred compensation, pension plan, a low-interest loan, liberal use of the company aircraft, plus many other privileges and perquisites that had been granted over the years by an appreciative board of directors. All of the details of the entire package had been given to the conglomerate by the consultant with his recommendations on the conditions that would be required to attract the executive. When the candidate signaled that he would consider an offer, the top management team of the conglomerate began to discuss the consultant's recommendations. Many executives were involved in the decision-making process, all of whom had heavy travel schedules. Despite the best efforts of the consultant, weeks went by with no decision on the conditions of a firm offer. The consultant periodically explained to the candidate the reasons for the delay.

Eleven weeks after he had indicated his willingness to consider an offer, the candidate told the consultant that he had just been approached by another company and that after only one meeting with their board of directors, they were making an offer. The conglomerate then scrambled to decide on a package. They were too late. The candidate was lost to the other company. The conglomerate eventually had to fill their position with an executive from a related but not the same industry.

The conglomerate and the consultant had done everything right up to the point of making an offer. However, during the process of persuading the candidate to consider the open position, they had opened his mind to the whole idea of making a change at that stage of his career. The candidate had confided in a few of his close friends, seeking their advice on the proposed move. One of these friends knew of the other company's decision to seek a new CEO, and made the connection.

When a candidate's interest in the open position has been brought to a point at which he is willing to consider an offer, time is of the essence. There should be no delay in presenting the proposed conditions of employment to him.

Many companies invest substantial effort, with their executive search consultant, in finding and persuading the ideal candidate and then lose him as a result of failure to continue to follow the consultant's advice during the negotiating phase of the recruitment process. They overlook the fact that executives who may be decisive in the performance of their jobs with their companies often find, nevertheless, that consideration of a change of companies is a traumatic experience. The trauma reaches its peak at the point at which an offer is presented and a decision has to be made. Delays, poor handling of the circumstances leading to the offer, and unskillful negotiations can easily discourage the candidate and increase the probability of his deciding to remain where he is or accept another position.

Another impediment to successful negotiation is the assumption on the part of the executives in the organization that candidates must demonstrate a very strong desire to be hired for the open position. It is often difficult for many executives to understand that the candidate is not seeking a change but was discovered, sought out, and persuaded by the consultant to explore the opportunity. Too frequently, good candidates are rejected because "he is not hungry enough" or "he is not keen enough about the job" or "he has not convinced me that he really wants to join us." When the decision is reached that an offer will be made, the candidate still usually has to be convinced and may not, at this stage, be displaying more than mild interest.

The position description and specification is discussed in Chapter Six. The quality of the thinking that was invested in its preparation will have a direct effect on the negotiations. The consultant will have tried to raise every conceivable question that may arise during negotiations with the candidate. To the extent to which they were thoroughly considered and answered in the position description, problems during negotiations will be reduced.

Negotiations with a candidate do not always begin only at the point at which he states that he is willing to consider an offer. The consultant will often have begun the process during his initial contacts and interview while acquainting the candidate with the position and gaining insights into his thinking about it and the compensation package.

There are four main areas that cause problems in negotiations with a candidate. One of these is the structuring of the position—the functions, responsibilities, authorities, accountabilities, and relationships. The second is the compensation package together with the perquisites and privileges. The third area is the obligations that the organization is willing to underwrite in connection with moving the family from the present home and location to another. Although the structure, the compensation package, and the conditions for the move will have been clearly spelled out in the position description prior to commencing the search, subsequent flexibility is often essential in attracting an outstanding executive. The fourth area is future opportunity within the organization. Certainly it would be unreasonable for the candidate to expect a firm commitment on future moves, but he will usually require a clear idea of the promotion paths that could be open to him if he earns them.

The structure of the position is sometimes changed during negotiations. In one company that was having a top executive search conducted, it had been traditional for the Chairman to have direct responsibility for research and development. The top candidate for the President position insisted that he would not accept the job, with its attendant responsibility for increasing the share of market, unless he had direct responsibility for all functions except the public relations and legal areas. In another case, it was customary for regional Vice Presidents to utilize the corporate headquarters marketing staff, but the best candidate for one of the regional positions refused to accept it unless he could have a Director of Marketing reporting directly to him. He made the point that the desired turnaround in the region that was suffering heavy losses could not be accomplished unless he had direct control over the marketing staff. In both cases, the companies acceded. In neither case had these issues surfaced until negotiations began because the candidates had not, until then, focused intensively on these positions.

The structure is often more difficult to negotiate when family-owned and -managed companies decide to fill the top position with an outsider. An experienced executive search consultant knows that long-standing internal relationships can make it impossible for the new CEO to function effectively. Both in privately and publicly held organizations, the consultant will often suggest a form of role playing or a "what if" exercise to help the company and the candidate to foresee and resolve potential problem situations prior to their signing an agreement.

Several years ago, the two aging owner-managers of a privately held company decided to take it easy and to bring in a professional CEO. They had both insisted, when the position description was being prepared, that they wanted to turn over the entire responsibility to the successful candidate. During the negotiations, the consultant suggested that they map out the type of organization structure that the candidate had in mind and then discuss the suitability of existing long-service executives for the positions in the reorganized company. This exercise stopped the negotiations cold. Only then did the owners realize that they were not ready to let someone else make changes that could displace old friends in the company. It was not until three years later, when the company was in trouble and one of the owners was ill, that they were willing to accept the reality of the need of a major overhaul.

The other area of negotiation, compensation—including benefits, perquisites, and privileges—is often more complex because there are so many components in the total package, and because any one of them can be an emotional rather than a logical issue on either side. A major defense against surprises when negotiations begin is the thoroughness of the consultant's report on the candidate's existing and desired package. The compensation section of the interview check list in Chapter Eight helps to ensure that no significant items are overlooked before negotiations begin. Of course, some candidates are reluctant to be specific about the details of what they would require, preferring to remain silent on that subject until an offer is forthcoming.

The "Harvard Offer" has proven to be a useful practice at this stage. The company and the consultant agree on a total package that should satisfy the candidate. The consultant then communicates the offer by asking the candidate, What would be your reaction if my client were to offer the following package to you? The consultant can then counsel both client and candidate before a formal offer is made.

A professional executive search consultant is guided by his main objective, i.e., to do what is best for both his client and his candidate. He must frankly tell his candidate when he is being unreasonable. He must pull no punches with his client when the offer is unrealistic. The consultant should stimulate creativity in developing mutually acceptable solutions.

When constructing compensation packages, companies too often suffer from preoccupation with their own viewpoints, tending to expect that anyone being invited to join them will somehow fit into their patterns. Frequently they are guided by survey data that reports on the current compensation of incumbents, ignoring the fact that to attract one of these incumbents they will probably have to offer a substantial premium.

Too often there is a failure to be realistic about the candidate's bottom line. Taking everything into consideration, how much better off would the candidate be financially and with respect to quality of life if he were to accept this offer? In addition to the executive search consultant's expertise, the answers to this complex question may require the advice of tax counsel plus the assistance of the company's own personal staff who are experts on local living conditions.

When the salary that would be required to attract an outstanding candidate exceeds the level permitted by the salary structure, rather than make an exception, companies often add a guaranteed bonus for the first year or two. The assumption is made that by the time that the guaranteed bonus ends, the executive's performance will have justified a larger bonus and an increase in salary. In addition, with increasing frequency, one-time, "up-front" bonuses are offered to tip the scale toward acceptance of the offer and to more adequately compensate the candidate for the inconvenience, cost, and risk of leaving his present employment.

The cash compensation is not always the main issue. Stock options in a company with a promising future can be far more attractive than larger current cash income. Quality of life, schooling, and climate have their effect on the rest of the package. Such apparently minor items as the type of company automobile, use of chauffeurs, the size, location, and decor of the proposed office, location of reserved parking space, clubs, executive dining room, executive fitness centers, and medical facilities all affect the attractiveness of the total package.

The image of the organization can be a major factor that influences the negotiations. One company that has a remarkable worldwide growth record and a reputation for excellence, periodically retains an executive search firm to fill vacancies. The company shuns impressive titles. Its offices are spartan. All executives travel coach class and stay in modest hotels. On the other hand, cash and deferred compensation, stock options, and benefits are above average. The combination of image and realistic compensation more than offset the lack of perquisites. The company usually succeeds in attracting the best, but not always. Some executives refuse to give up perquisites and privileges to which they have become accustomed.

Spouses and families are too often overlooked until negotiations have reached an advanced stage. They may have been persuaded by the candidate to accept the possibility of the change in principle, but when a firm decision is about to be or has been made by the candidate, the spouse or family sometimes rebel. The causes are many, ranging from the spouse's employment, professional or community activities, opposition to yet another move, or the possible adverse effects on children's education. In one case, the wife's substantial income from a large inheritance was not taken into consideration when calculating the tax effects of moving from one country to another. The executive search consultant can substantially reduce these unpleasant surprises by ensuring that the spouse and family are involved in the decision making at the right stage in the discussions with the candidate.

Executives in the U.S. often say that employment contracts are rare in the U.S. but are common in Europe. Although the conditions may differ, the fact is that every employment agreement is a contract. Therefore, contracts are a normal part of negotiations with executives anywhere. They are a means of stating in writing the conditions of employment that have been accepted by the candidate. While such formal agreements in Europe usually include guaranteed lengthy periods of employment with long notice of termination periods by either party, in the U.S. and elsewhere, they may be more concerned with conditions for compensating the candidate for lost stock options and deferred compensation as a result of moving from one company to another. Agreements may include conditions under which the selling and buying of houses, the cost of moving, and the provision of interest-free loans and of special bonuses are offered. All contracts should include the full details of all forms of compensation, benefits, and perquisites as well as minimum notice of termination periods for either party, and they must, of course, adhere to the laws and regulations of the country, state, or city in which the contract is drawn.

Throughout the process of assessing the candidate and negotiating with him, judgment, under the guidance of the consultant, will be exercised as to whether the candidate is acting in good faith or is playing games to enhance his self-esteem and to put him in a strong position to negotiate with his present employer. This problem is explored further in the next chapter.

Despite the best efforts of everyone, some negotiations will fail. The consultant will usually, in the meantime, have maintained communications with the one or two other active candidates. In the aftermath of the disappointment over the rejection by the first candidate, there is sometimes a tendency to drop the other candidates and to start all over again. This is usually a mistake because the other candidates are the result of an intensive search and a careful selection process. The second choice often turns out to be more reasonable in negotiations and highly effective in the new job.

The partnership between the organization and the executive search consultant, to which reference has been made in previous chapters, is just as essential to success during the negotiating phase as it is throughout the other steps in the entire process. Confidence in the consultant's judgment and integrity is especially important during negotiations. The partnership should result in negotiations that produce optimum conditions for both the organization and the candidate.

Chapter Eleven

Separating
the Selected Executive
From His
Present Organization

After four months of effort beginning with the discussion of the specifications of the executive to fill the position, and continuing through the searching, interviewing, and negotiating, the ideal executive had signed the contract and had given his company 30 days notice. Within a few days, he explained that his company had asked him to stay on board for another six months to train his replacement, but he persuaded them to reduce the period to three months. The organization that was hiring him expressed concern over the inconvenience that would be caused by the delay, but agreed that he should try to leave his present employer under positive conditions. During those three months, the executive was invited to select the furniture and decor of his new office, and his new company car. Announcements of his appointment had appeared in the press and in the company house organ. Steps to sell his home and purchase a new one were to be delayed until closer to the end of the school year when the family would move. Finally, the starting date, February 1st, arrived, and the key executives of the new employer were ready to greet their new Vice President. He never arrived. Instead, at 10 A.M. that morning, he called the President and explained that he had been in an all night marathon session with his President and other board members during which new conditions were offered to him that he would have been foolish to reject. He explained further that during the past month, his wife and children had expressed increasing dismay over the move. He requested that the contract that he had signed three months earlier be cancelled. Seven months after commencing the project to fill the position, the company had to start all over again.

What went wrong? Is it possible to prevent such events from occurring? There is no guarantee that such happenings can be averted but an experienced professional executive search consultant can help you to substantially reduce the chances of an experience of this kind. In this case, the company had taken many of the right steps. They had not, however, taken some precautionary measures that a good executive search consultant would have insisted upon.

During the interviewing and assessing of the prospective candidate, the consultant is exercising judgment on the probability of attracting him to the open position. The first criterion is whether the proposed move would be in the best interests of the candidate, taking everything—including career, personal, and family factors—into consideration. Unless the conclusion is positive, the prospective candidate should be dropped, thereby eliminating one major reason for a last-minute reversal or worse still, his joining and then leaving a year later, having realized that he had made a wrong move.

As the exploration between candidate and organization proceeds, judgment is exercised, guided by the consultant, on the depth and seriousness of the candidate's interest. Is he motivated by the flattery of being sought after? Is he mainly interested in finding out how much he is worth? Is he developing a case that he can use to negotiate better conditions with his present employer?

A distinction needs to be made between lack of interest in the proposed position and inappropriateness of the proposed change. It is in the latter case that efforts to recruit the executive should be dropped. But if the move would be right for both parties but the executive lacks interest, then, as explained in Chapter Ten, you and the consultant can work together to help the executive to change his mind. Only when it is apparent that the candidate and his family are firmly convinced, should he be invited to sign a contract. By following this ground rule, the chances of a subsequent change of mind are reduced.

Recently, the Board of Directors of a medium-sized company in the

Northeast reached the painful conclusion that although their 63-year-old CEO was an outstanding producer of growth and profits, he had been unable to select and develop a successor. The CEO was scheduled to retire at age 65. The corporate Vice President Marketing had been terminated. The Board decided to recruit a new CEO, initially placing the candidate in the Vice President Marketing position but guaranteeing him the CEO position within 18 months when the present CEO would retire.

An executive search firm was retained. Within six weeks the consultant and the board had agreed upon three candidates. One of them was a young General Manager of a major division of a company in a similar industry. He had a strong marketing background. As his attitude was changed from only mild interest to enthusiasm, all of the right steps were taken, including ensuring that his family shared his interest in the move. A point was reached at which the consultant made a "Harvard Offer," i.e., he asked the candidate what would be his reaction if his client were to offer the following conditions of employment to him. The candidate responded positively with two minor exceptions that the consultant was certain could be easily resolved.

The stage was then set for a most important exercise in reducing the chances of the candidate subsequently backing out. The consultant introduced a mild form of role playing. He described to the candidate a scene in which he asked the candidate to imagine that the consultant was the candidate's present boss. He asked the candidate to describe how he would communicate to his boss his decision to resign.

The candidate and his boss were old friends. In the role playing, the candidate started out by saying, "Joe, I have an important matter to discuss with you and I want to ask your advice on it as an old friend." The consultant, acting as the boss, when he was told by the candidate about the intended resignation, immediately strongly advised him against it, giving numerous reasons for his friendly advice. The candidate could go no further. The consultant was then able to impress upon the candidate that a resignation has to be handled in the same decisive, firm, businesslike manner in which the candidate would conduct himself in all other important business events.

Next came part two of the role playing in which the consultant asked the candidate to imagine another scene three weeks later. In the meantime, said the consultant, "Let us imagine that your boss, several other top executives, your peers and your subordinates have all increased their efforts to persuade you to stay. Now, in the third week, the boss takes you and your wife to dinner and announces that the company has decided to advance, by six months, the promotion that they had planned for you to fill a newly created Vice President position with responsibility for three divisions, a substantial increase in salary, stock options, and bonus opportunity." The consultant then asks the candidate how he and his wife would respond to such a proposal. In this case, the candidate immediately said that he would politely but firmly reject the offer because it would be quite apparent that his boss had persuaded his company to create a situation for the sole purpose of making it attractive enough for the candidate to remain with his present company. After some further probing, the consultant was satisfied that the candidate would probably not change his mind if he were to accept an offer from his client. Nevertheless, the consultant impressed two considerations upon the candidate. The most important of these was that if he were to allow himself to be persuaded to stay, his image within his present company would be tarnished, mainly due to the fact that he had made a commitment that he had failed to honor but also because he had displayed disloyalty. The other consideration was the damage that would be sustained to the candidate's reputation outside his company. The failure by an executive to honor an important commitment is news that spreads far and wide.

In this case, the candidate accepted the offer. Subsequently his employer went to even greater lengths to change his mind than had been envisaged in the role playing. The consultant and executives of the company that the candidate was to join kept in close, constant touch with the candidate, including additional visits to the headquarters for briefings, for finding a new home, and for socializing. The candidate resisted all efforts to change his mind and joined the company on schedule.

An experienced executive search consultant knows that most candidates need guidance in the art of terminating their employment with their present organizations. Usually there are close and meaningful interpersonal relationships with the people whom the candidate will be leaving. To break away elegantly, avoiding enmity and recriminations while being forthright and businesslike is often one of the more difficult challenges that the candidate has encountered in his career. Your consultant can make the whole process much easier for the candidate, enabling him to join your organization with a positive, enthusiastic attitude.

Chapter Twelve

The Search Firm's Role After the Executive Has Joined Your Organization

When the candidate arrives at your office for his first day on the job with your organization, should your communications with your executive search consultant come to an end on this particular assignment, other than to settle the final invoice for his services and expenses? Having hired the candidate and brought him aboard, should you assume that the responsibility for the successful integration of the candidate into your organization is entirely yours from now on, with no further involvement of the consultant? The answer to these questions is a resounding NO!

The partnership between you and the consultant began when you and he agreed to work together to solve your executive vacancy problem. That partnership should not be terminated until both of you are reasonably certain that the problem has been solved. Neither of you can rest assured of success until the candidate is fully integrated into your organization and is performing successfully.

Here again is a clear example of the difference between recruiters, headhunters, and a professional executive search firm. If you give your executive vacancy problem to a firm that views its role as "supplying a warm body," your relationship with that firm probably came to an end at the moment that your candidate signed on, and you paid the bill. The professional executive search consultant, although no longer receiving a retainer from you, will continue the partnership with you as long as is necessary to ensure that your executive vacancy problem has been solved.

No matter how thoroughly all of the steps in the recruitment process have been handled, the period during which the candidate is becoming an integral part of your organization is risky and requires the same careful thought and attention as has been given to all of the other steps. There may be a honeymoon period during which the new executive is not expected to perform but only to learn. Sooner or later, he will be judged not only on his behavior but on performance and results. During his first year, it is essential that he receive more than the usual guidance and feedback. But too often, because he is new, there is a tendency to avoid frank discussion with him, and he is left with the assumption that he is doing well, while behind his back there may be growing criticisms. This process can reach a crescendo in which negative attitudes toward the new man have become so firmly established that there is no hope of changing them, and the executive who was such a promising candidate has to leave.

A large company in the industrial products field had never before brought an executive in from outside the organization to fill a senior level vacancy. The sudden death of the President of their largest division led to the conclusion that none of the executives who were being developed for that position were ready for it. They retained an executive search firm to help them to fill the vacancy. Within one month, they were introduced to the first candidate. Their immediate conclusion was that he was ideal. They did not want to see anyone else. He was offered the position but firmly decided not to accept it because he felt uneasy about the personal chemistry between himself and some of the executives with whom he would work. The search continued and other well-qualified candidates were presented. None of them, in the opinion of company executives, quite measured up to the first candidate. After seven months of effort, the consultant, who had kept in periodic touch with the first candidate, returned to him and persuaded him to reconsider. There were several meetings between him, the President, the Chairman and other executives of the company that finally, eleven months after he was first introduced, resulted in acceptance by the first candidate. One month later, he joined the company.

The candidate had an excellent track record. He was known to be thoughtful and decisive. In the new company, during his first year, he was cautious while he familiarized himself with an entirely different environment. He was slow to make decisions and, in the process, asked for large quantities of detailed information and had numerous meetings with line and staff executives. Within three months of his joining, criticism of his style began to grow. The Chairman became especially negative, while the President, to whom the executive reported, was his only staunch supporter. By the end of the first year, the general opinion, not shared by the President, was that the new man would have to be replaced. However, no one had given the new executive any feedback whatsoever. The President could see no faults in him or his performance. The Chairman, to avoid unpleasantness, did not push his opinions with the President, and would not go around him to talk frankly with the executive. Other executives in the organization said nothing to the new man, believing that it was not politic to do so when the President obviously regarded the man so highly. The consultant, during that first year, tried repeatedly to help to resolve the problem, but the Chairman would not allow the consultant to talk frankly either to the President or to the new executive.

Although the division for which the new executive was responsible was meeting all of the established targets, the negative attitudes of the Chairman and other executives became more evident. The new executive, despite encouragement by the President, became increasingly aware of what had then become a hostile atmosphere. He had not quite completed his second year when he resigned and returned to his former company. The consultant was strongly of the opinion that the executive and the company would have adapted to each other if there had been frank discussions between them from the beginning. He pointed out that there had never been a single criticism conveyed to the new executive by anyone, not even when he had asked his President for opinions of his performance. On the contrary, based upon the performance of the division, he had been given an increase in salary, a substantial bonus, and additional stock options.

The executives of the company had failed to recognize that adaptation to a new corporate environment takes time and requires patience as well as understanding. In this case, the candidate, in his previous organization, had a reputation for being a dynamic leader who made excellent decisions without hesitation. However, there was a vast difference between an environment in which he knew his superiors and peers very well and had built his own team versus the new organization in which everyone above, at the same level, and below him were strangers. He had modified his behavior while he tried to learn his way around in the new, complex maze, thus giving the impression that he was overly cautious, indecisive, and too preoccupied with details. The fact was that no one was giving him any guidance, thus prolonging the adaptation period until it failed. The consultant, in this case, was not assiduous enough in defining the problem, explaining it to his client, and persuading them to take action.

This is not an isolated case. While not a substantial percentage of executives brought in from the outside actually leave within two years, it happens often enough to emphasize the importance of treating the integration period as part of the recruitment process and to give it the well-organized, thoughtful attention that it deserves. Even if the new man does not leave, the first two years can be unpleasant and costly when the basic rules of good management are ignored or avoided.

One way of dealing with this problem is to schedule a monthly review during the first year and a quarterly review during the second year during which there is frank two-way discussion of behavior, performance, and results as viewed by all concerned. Admittedly, this procedure is time-consuming and difficult to schedule, but the alternative of the risk of losing a good executive and going through the whole process again of replacing him justifies the extra effort.

Chapter Thirteen

How to Evaluate
the Performance
of Your Executive
Search Firm

The previous ten chapters of this book describe, in detail, how executive search firms should behave and perform. After the candidate has joined your organization, you and the other executives who were involved in working with your executive search firm will undoubtedly comment on its performance. You may find it useful to gather these comments on a more formal basis to develop a comprehensive assessment of the firm and of the consultant who was mainly responsible for your assignment. The assessment can be used to decide whether to use the firm again and if so, to provide guidance that could improve the firm's performance on future assignments. Discussion of your assessment with the firm will give them an opportunity to comment on how you and your organization could improve your role throughout the various steps from the beginning to the end of the project. The following guidelines are intended to serve as reminders of the criteria on which to base your judgments.

1. To begin at the beginning, how clearly did the executive search consultant explain:

   The estimated duration of the search

All of the steps of the search and the extent of the firm's involvement in each step

The details of their system of charging for their services and expenses

Whether and how they would continue to charge for their services if the assignment were prolonged far beyond the estimated duration

What they would charge if you hired a second candidate as a result of the search

What arrangement they would propose in the event that their candidate subsequently leaves or is terminated by your company

Their policy on taking executives from their clients

Which companies in your industry are their clients and the extent to which they are blocked from taking people from those companies

Who will actually handle the search

The extent to which their research department will be involved in the search

If the search involves other countries, exactly how will the work in those countries be conducted

2. During the next step, when you were communicating to the search firm the description of the vacant position and your thoughts on the executive who would be required to fill it, did the firm simply accept what you told them or did they probe deeply, discuss, and counsel with you until there was a very clear meeting of the minds?

Did you begin to have a sense of partnership with the consultant at that stage?

Did the consultant submit a draft position description and specification to you for discussion and approval? What was your opinion of the quality of his draft?

3. After the search commenced, what was your opinion of the frequency of the consultant's discussions with you of prospec-

tive candidates whom he was considering. What did you think of the quality of those discussions? Did the sense of partnership continue to develop?

4. As the search progressed, were you positively impressed by the breadth of coverage? Were you satisfied that the strategy and its implementation would maximize the chances of finding the best candidate for your particular requirements? Did you feel that the consultant was more interested in placing a candidate with you rather than developing the optimum solution to your executive vacancy problem?

5. During the process of deciding on which prospective candidates should actually be considered by you as candidates, did the consultant convince you that he had thoroughly evaluated the candidates?

   Did he limit his recommendations to three candidates or did he try to impress you by supplying quantity rather than quality? Did you continue to feel that you and the consultant were working together as partners at this stage?

6. Did the consultant arrange the interviews for you efficiently? Did he offer to be present at every interview?

7. How objective and helpful was the consultant during the process of deciding on which candidate to select? When the decision was made, how skillfully did he handle the other candidates in either rejecting them altogether or keeping them available on the sidelines?

8. During negotiations with the selected candidate, did the consultant fulfill his role effectively? How well did he maintain a proper balance between your company's interests and those of the candidate? To what extent did he offer creative solutions to problems?

9. Did he provide effective guidance to you and the candidate during the period of the candidate's resignation and departure from his company?

10. Did he skillfully sign off the candidates who were not selected?

11. If the selected candidate backed out, was it due to lack of effectiveness on the consultant's part? How well did he handle the development of an alternative candidate?

12. Is he keeping in touch with you and the candidate now that the candidate has joined your organization?

13. Were the search firm's invoices for services and expenses in accordance with your understanding of the business arrangement?

14. How well did the consultant manage the entire project? Did he keep it moving at an acceptable pace? Was it completed within a reasonable period?

15. If there were undue delays, did the consultant discuss these with you in a timely and frank manner? Did he offer a billing arrangement that was reasonable under the circumstances?

16. Taking into consideration the thoroughness of the search, the consultant's attentiveness, his energy level, his availability, professional standards, and continuity, how would you rate his overall performance?

OUTSTANDING
EXCELLENT
GOOD
FAIR
POOR

17. Would you recommend that he be retained again by your organization?

If your overall rating is Outstanding or Excellent, you will have established a relationship with a search firm and a search consultant that can be invaluable to you when other executive vacancies occur. They already know your organization and have proven that they understand the human chemistry that fits. Usually, you can be reasonably confident that the same standards of performance will be applied to future assignments, although you will still be well advised to review the track record and reputation of the consultant proposed for the next assignment if he is not the same person who handled your previous project.

When the rating is Good or Fair, it may be worthwhile to have a thorough, frank discussion of the criticisms. Depending upon the outcome, you may decide that, given the time and effort already invested in working with the search firm, they should be given an opportunity to prove that they can improve their performance.

Chapter Fourteen

Solving the Special Problems Encountered by Organizations in Using Executive Search Firms

There are 13 complaints that are most frequently voiced by organizations that retain executive search firms.

1. The consultant does not understand our requirement

A company on the West Coast had retained a search firm to fill their Vice President Marketing position. The President and the Vice President Human Resources had explained the details of the job, the specifications for the candidate, and had provided the consultant with substantial, well-prepared written material.

The consultant, over the next few weeks, discussed a number of potential candidates, most of whose backgrounds conformed very well to the specifications. Three of these candidates were selected to be interviewed by the Vice President Human Resources. After spending several hours with each of them, his conclusion was that they were "not sharp enough," but nevertheless, he introduced them to the President. The President fully concurred with his Vice President's opinion.

The consultant then presented two more candidates. They were also rejected for the same reason—"not sharp enough." At this point, the head of the search firm stepped in. He quickly realized that there must be a key ingredient that was missing in the consultant's understanding of the job. He questioned at length both the President and the Vice President on their meaning of the expression "not sharp enough."

The company, in this case, was unusually numbers oriented. All of their executives had very quick minds with figures. The importance of this factor was never mentioned in either the written material or during the conversations between the company and the consultant because company executives took this characteristic for granted. Under these circumstances, the Vice President and the President, during the interviews, found that the candidates did not respond impressively to many of their questions that tended to be numbers oriented, and simply concluded that the candidates were "not sharp enough." However, when the head of the search firm questioned them, it became apparent that the missing ingredient was "must be unusually strong in finance; must come from a company that has a highly sophisticated business planning system."

Although the company should have included this important requirement in the specification, the fault in this case lies mainly with the search consultant who failed to ask the right questions before the search commenced. An executive search will almost certainly fail unless there is a thorough understanding between the organization and the consultant, at the outset, of the organization, the open position, and the executive required to fill it.

2. The consultant fails to understand the human chemistry in our organization

The President of the health care products division of a multinational corporation agreed with his Vice President Personnel that they would retain an executive search firm to replace their Vice President in charge of their diagnostics division, who had been fired. The President was extremely bright, with an unusually dry sense of humor. He demanded that those who worked with him must be brief and to the point. He was physically very fit and a nonsmoker. He was an exceptionally well-disciplined person.

During the four weeks after accepting the assignment, the consultant discussed several prospective candidates as a result of which two were selected for presentation to the Vice President Personnel. Both candidates had exactly the right education and experience. Both were rejected within 10 minutes by the Vice President Personnel. Both were flamboyant, talkative, heavy smokers who were intelligent enough to do their current jobs but were not exceptional.

The Vice President Personnel had not spelled out all of the characteristics required because (1) he was not asked by the consultant and (2) he assumed that an experienced consultant, after spending an hour with the President of the division, would have understood at least the fundamental characteristics that would not fit the organization. Had the consultant probed and perhaps met some of the other executives reporting to the Division President, he would not have presented people who could not possibly become a member of his client's team.

3. The consultant is obviously overloaded

It is sometimes true that consultants become overloaded. If properly spaced, a consultant can effectively handle six assignments at a time in the United States and perhaps more in countries in which industry and commerce are concentrated in one or two cities. Some consultants undertake more than they can handle effectively. Others, at times, experience an overload because one or more of their nearly completed assignments go sour and have to be redone. The result of the overload is an increase in the time span needed to accomplish each step or a drop in the quality of the work.

Complaints about overloading are, in many cases, not justified. Some organizations make unreasonable demands on the consultant's time. As an average, each assignment requires about 150 man-hours of a consultant's time, spread over a period of about five months from the beginning of the assignment until the candidate joins the client organization. However, some clients behave as though they have the consultant under contract on a full-time basis during this period.

Whether the complaint appears to be caused by the organization or by the consultant, the main solution to the problem lies in establishing the close working partnership that is so essential to a good executive search project right from the outset. Checking out the search firm and the consultant beforehand will also reduce the likelihood of retaining a consultant who does not maintain his workload within manageable limits.

4. The consultant has not conducted a thorough search

When there is an understanding, before the search starts or during its early stages, on the strategy and scope that will be applied, and if the consultant is in weekly contact with you, the likelihood of there being a justified complaint of failure to conduct the search thoroughly is minimized.

In one case, a search consultant accepted an assignment to fill the position of Vice President and General Manager of the automotive accessories division of a conglomerate. The consultant was familiar with the industry and knew of two well-qualified executives who would be interested. He presented them to his client. His client agreed that the candidates were excellent but insisted on seeing more. The consultant told them that there was no one else as well qualified to whom the open position would be attractive. The client produced a list of all of their competitors and demanded a report from the consultant on the results of his exploration of each company on the list. The consultant explained that due to his knowledge of their industry and his numerous reliable sources of information on executives in that industry, it had not been necessary to systematically investigate every competitor. The client finally hired one of the two candidates, but said that they would not retain that consultant nor his firm again.

Had the company and the consultant had a frank discussion on strategy and scope during the early stages, it is probable that there would have been no such complaints when the assignment was successfully completed.

5. The consultant was arrogant

As in any profession, there is a wide range of behavior among executive search consultants. There are some who believe that as top professionals in their field, when they advise a client to hire a particular executive for a position, the client should do so without question. If the client disagrees, these consultants become very insistent. Some of these consultants have a good record of completing a high percentage of their assignments, and in record time.

At the other end of the spectrum, there are executive search consultants who make no effort to convince their clients that they should hire their candidates. Some of them simply continue to present candidates until one of them is hired. Their batting average is not usually so good.

The behavior of most good executive search consultants is somewhere between these two extremes. Prior to retaining a consultant, you can find out whether his perception of his role suits you.

6. The consultant inflated the compensation package

Most search firms express their service charges as a percentage of the gross annual compensation of the executives whom they place in their client organizations. This formula sometimes causes the client to suspect that the consultant is pushing the compensation as high as possible for his own benefit. Another reason for such suspicions is the fact that higher compensation levels make it easier for the consultant to attract good executives.

On the other hand, organizations are often unreasonable when establishing the compensation package for a position to be filled from the outside. A typical example is an assignment to fill the position of Vice President Europe for a U.S. multinational corporation. The client used survey data for their industry and insisted that the starting compensation for this position would have to fall within the lower third of the survey range. But they also specified that candidates must have had area management responsibility in Europe in the same industry. Obviously, it was unlikely that an executive who is already at the Area Vice President level in the same industry in Europe could be attracted to a similar position with a competitor at a compensation level within the lower third of the average range for that industry in Europe.

Some consultants will finally accept an assignment under these conditions, rationalizing that they can subsequently demonstrate that their client must either pay a premium to attract a good executive into a lateral move, or the client must lower the specifications so that executives for whom the open position would be a promotion can be considered. This is an unwise decision because it usually destroys the kind of close working relationship governed by mutual trust and confidence that is such an important ingredient of a successful executive search project. The wisest course of action is for both you and the consultant to agree that you will be governed by the marketplace. A sensible target compensation level can be agreed upon and be kept in mind, but highly qualified candidates who would require higher compensation will be discussed with you so that you can decide whether to give them further consideration.

7. The consultant failed to thoroughly check the candidate's background

The policies and practices of executive search firms vary on reference checking and background investigation. There are those who believe that such checking should be the responsibility of the client. There are other search firms that take full responsibility for ensuring that their clients will not experience any unpleasant surprises due to lack of important information after their candidates are hired. If this latter policy is what you want, you need only make this clear to the consultant before you engage him and then accept nothing less.

The difficulties of making confidential inquiries about an executive who is currently employed and who is not seeking a change are quite severe. There is also the danger that an outstanding prospect might be rejected by the consultant because of a negative reference, whereas a more complete and balanced investigation would reveal that, being a strong executive, the prospect had made some enemies who would have nothing good to say about him, but that majority opinion was quite positive. Sometimes the opposite happens. Just one extremely positive reference can cause such a strong bias in favor of a prospect that no further investigation is conducted. The likelihood of your losing the opportunity to consider an outstanding executive when the consultant has obtained a bad reference or of hiring a candidate who has not been checked out thoroughly, can be reduced by your establishing a clear understanding with your consultant on your standards and degree of flexibility.

Reference checking and background investigation are part of the whole process of assessing an executive. Executive assessment requires strong professional competence. This is one of the most important considerations when you are selecting and working with an executive search consultant.

8. The consultant was of little help during the negotiations with the candidate

Some organizations are of the opinion that the executive search consultant should not be involved in negotiations. Others depend heavily on the consultant during negotiations. The fact is that you have engaged the consultant to help you to solve your executive vacancy problem. Negotiation is a critical phase of the whole project and sometimes begins with the consultant's first contact with the candidate. As a professional third party, the consultant can play an invaluable role in helping you and the candidate to reach agreement. However, if you have, in your organization, a personnel executive who is skilled in executive negotiations, you may prefer to delegate that role entirely to him.

In a recent case, an extensive search on behalf of a European company finally produced an ideal candidate for the position of President of their large U.S. subsidiary. The Chairman of the parent company personally handled the negotiations and failed. He agreed to let the consultant try to reopen the discussions. It took several weeks for the consultant to gradually bring about compromises. The consultant was so certain that the move would be right for both his client and his candidate that he was able to convince them both that they should be more flexible. The candidate finally accepted.

Normally, in arranging to retain an executive search firm, you reach an understanding with them on their role in the negotiation phase of the project. If you want the consultant to be involved, you would be well advised to ensure that he has a proven record of successful negotiation and that he customarily works closely with his clients on candidate negotiations.

9. The consultant ignored us after the candidate accepted our offer

There are two final steps in an executive search project. One of them is to ensure that the candidate successfully resigns his present position. The other is to ensure that the integration of the candidate into the organization is accomplished without serious problems. The consultant's experience and talents are usually needed for both of these steps. This fact should be part of your understanding with the consultant before the search begins.

10. The consultant tried to overcharge us

Reputable executive search firms state, in writing, their system of charges. The only three possibilities for misunderstanding then are the compensation package on which the total service charge will be based, the amount and frequency of the retainer payments, and the expense charges.

Most search firms express their total service charge as a percentage of annual compensation. Others establish a fixed charge. The definition of annual compensation, when the percentage method is used, is normally base salary plus estimated bonus for the first twelve months. There are exceptions in cases in which the compensation package is designed for start-up or turnaround, with a lower or no salary but high stock options and future bonus opportunity. In any case, by clearly spelling out the basis for calculating the total service charge, there should not be a misunderstanding.

The same applies to the retainers. The search firm will normally spell out the frequency and amount of the retainers that it will charge and that will be credited against the basic charge, and will tell you, in writing, whether or not the retainer charges may exceed the amount of the basic charge. They will also discuss expense charges with you and will explain in advance, for example, if they expect to incur unusually high telephone charges because the search is international. Normally they will clear proposed substantial travel with you beforehand.

In other words, the standard practices of good, sound, professional executive search firms should eliminate any reason for complaints about excessive charges.

11. A search firm recruited one of our executives after we had become a client of theirs

This is a problem that is the subject of much discussion among executive search consultants. For example, search firms that operate in several countries do not usually commit themselves to protecting a client worldwide just because they have served that client in one country. The same principle applies when only one division of a conglomerate retains a search firm. However, the ethics of the executive search profession demand that a search firm must not use the information that it receives from a client organization to subsequently recruit from that organization.

In working with a reputable search firm, you can eliminate confusion over their policy on protecting your organization from recruiting your executives by asking them to discuss their policy with you and confirm it to you in writing.

12. The search took far too long

Some search assignments take longer than others because they prove to be more difficult. However, the prolongation of most searches occurs for either of two reasons. One is that the consultant is overloaded with other assignments. The other reason is that the client organization is slow in arranging interviews and making decisions.

These two main reasons can be avoided by establishing and maintaining a close working relationship with your search consultant. You can then frankly discuss his progress week by week, and he can encourage you and your organization to avoid delays and to understand the costly consequences of delays.

13. The search firm presented only one really good candidate

During a search for the President of a medium-sized consumer products company, the search consultant recommended three executives, all of whom were well qualified. The people in the client organization were lukewarm about the first two of these executives but had a very strong positive reaction to the third. They insisted on seeing more candidates. This took much more time. They were not enthusiastic about the additional candidates and were about to make an offer to their No. 1 choice when they learned that he had been promoted and was no longer a candidate. They decided to cancel the search and to promote one of their own people into the open position. They accused the search firm of recommending only one really good candidate.

The consultant and the client did not work closely enough together. Had they done so, the preferred candidate probably would have been hired without delay. Also, there was an overreaction to the No. 1 candidate that caused the people in the client organization to compare all other candidates to him superficially. Although the others were at least as well qualified, they had different personalities. They should have been given more thoughtful consideration.

Too often, organizations make the mistake of assuming that they are not receiving their money's worth unless their executive search consultant presents a large number of candidates to them. Rarely is there a bountiful supply of really good executives for any position. You and your search consultant can jointly decide, as the search progresses, which of the prospects whom he is considering should become candidates. In this way, you will know how thoroughly he is searching, and you will have a balanced view of the availability of good candidates. Provided that you have selected a good consultant and have followed the guidelines in this book for working with your consultant, there should be no cause for complaining that there were too few good candidates.

The causes of all 13 of these complaints can be avoided. The close working partnership between you and the consultant that has been emphasized throughout this book will eliminate or minimize these problems.

Chapter Fifteen

Some Common Problems Encountered by Executive Search Firms in Seeking to Provide Optimum Service

These are some of the problems with which search firms contend while trying to implement their professional role and maintain high ethical and performance standards.

1. Confusing executive search firms with recruiters and employment agencies

Executive search consultants receive calls or letters constantly from well-meaning friends and acquaintances to recommend an executive who is seeking a job or from the job-seeking executives themselves. They are surprised and perhaps offended when there is no invitation for an immediate interview but instead they are politely informed that "his background is not appropriate for any of our current assignments but we would be pleased to have his résumé on file for future reference." Many people assume that executive search firms are in the business of placing executives, whereas they are professional consultants retained by organizations to solve executive vacancy problems. There is still a widely held misconception that whenever a search consultant hears of a good executive who is available, he picks up the phone and calls several companies until he finds one with an opening into which the job-seeking executive would fit. This is definitely not the case.

These same people and others also believe that search firms fill executive vacancies by punching a computer keyboard and producing several résumés from the stored data on job-seeking executives. Some find it hard to believe that the data from the computer is merely one of many sources of information that search firms use when establishing the strategy for and conducting the search, and that a very high percentage of the executives who are placed by search firms were not seeking another job.

2. Client sets impossible standards

There is the old joke about the President who wants a Vice President position filled from outside his organization by an executive who has at least 20 years experience in a similar role, has a Master's degree but must be less than 40 years of age. There is a tendency on the part of some organizations to fail to distinguish between essential and desirable specifications. Those that try to set impossible standards are usually the ones who want it all at a salary that would hardly attract someone with minimal qualifications.

In some cases, there is a tendency to assume that because a search firm is being paid substantial retainers, they should be given specifications and limited to compensation packages that the organization itself knows to be next to impossible.

Executive searches are unlikely to succeed unless there is reasonableness, practicality, frankness, and flexibility in the relationship between client and consultant.

3. Clients have their own candidate

A good executive search consultant can usually obtain most of the information needed about his client's organization and the vacant position. There are some areas of information, however, that he could not know about unless his client cooperates. One of these is the existence of a candidate who was developed either internally or externally prior to the commencement of work by the search firm. In certain instances, the executives of an organization may be uncertain about their own candidate and may decide to have a search conducted so that they can compare their own candidate with those developed by the search firm. This is a sensible arrangement. Some such organizations fully inform the search firm of their strategy. They ask the consultant to assess their candidate, and they arrange to pay the search firm the full service charge even if their own candidate fills the position. In this way, the client organization establishes a close working partnership with the consultant and recognizes that the objective of the consultant's role is to help the organization to find the best solution to their executive vacancy problem, no matter who found the candidate.

Unfortunately, there are those organizations that do not understand this role and choose to hide the fact that they have their own candidate. This puts the search consultant at a disadvantage because he does not know with whom his candidates are being compared. Furthermore, such searches are often abruptly cancelled after the organization has seen one or two candidates and has decided to hire their own, whereas, had they gone through the entire process with their consultant, they could have increased their chances of filling the position with the best possible candidate.

A similar problem that often occurs is reflected in the case of an industrial products company in the Northeast that retained an international executive search firm to fill their vacant General Manager position in the United Kingdom. The company and the consultant had agreed that candidates must have a proven successful general management track record in the United Kingdom. In slightly less than four weeks after it began, the company cancelled the search and informed the consultant that they had found a candidate themselves and had hired him. The consultant was astonished when the successful candidate was identified. He was well known to the consultant and had not been recommended to the company because of dishonesty and marital problems. The company subsequently terminated the executive and asked the same search firm to replace him. The high direct and indirect cost of their mistake would have been avoided had they referred their candidate to the search consultant who would have informed them of the negative information. Had their candidate been well qualified, the consultant would have compared him to the other candidates and made his recommendation accordingly. If the company's candidate had been selected as the best, the search consultant could have assisted with the negotiations, counseling on the resignation and the other steps in the overall service to his client.

4. Client tries to use more than one search firm for the same assignment

An international executive search firm had been working for four weeks on an assignment to fill the position of President of the international division of a company when a recruiting firm heard about the search. They obtained an introduction to the Chief Executive Officer (CEO) and convinced him that they were so strong in the international field that they could develop the optimum candidate within three weeks. They offered to do this on a contingent basis. The CEO decided to accept. He reasoned that without paying additional retainers, he could have the services of two firms, thus increasing his chances of finding the best candidate.

In the meantime, the search firm had succeeded in persuading an outstanding international executive to explore the opportunity with their client. They were in the process of arranging with the executive to have a confidential meeting with their client, when the executive suddenly called and refused to go any further. His reason was that he had been contacted by a recruiter for the same position. He bluntly told the search consultant that confidentiality had been breached and that he would have nothing to do with a company that would handle high-level delicate contacts in such a manner. The ideal candidate was lost. The search firm informed their client that they would discontinue work on the assignment unless they cancelled their arrangement with the recruiting firm.

Reputable executive search firms will not handle assignments on which other firms are working. This is because prospective candidates who are hard to persuade will refuse to go further if they are contacted by more than one firm. Furthermore, confidentiality is much more difficult to maintain under such circumstances. In addition, if both firms recommend the same candidate, which of them should complete the other steps necessary to place him and which firm is paid for filling the position?

5. Client makes subsequent changes in specifications

During an executive search, as prospective candidates are being discussed and interviewed, client organizations sometimes change their minds about the specifications and, in some cases, even the organizational structure. In one case, there had been an argument going on for years about the structure of the marketing organization. The company had always had Vice Presidents of both marketing and sales reporting to the President.

The forthcoming retirement of the Vice President Marketing finally led to the conclusion that his replacement should be brought in from outside the company and that the new executive would be responsible for both sales and marketing. An executive search firm was retained. During the following six weeks, several people were discussed with the President and finally three were interviewed. While the President was trying to decide which was the best candidate, he learned that his Vice President Sales was actively seeking opportunities with other companies. The President suddenly changed his mind about the new organizational structure, called in the Vice President Sales, informed him that he would continue to report to the President, and obtained a commitment from him to remain with the company. Then the President informed the search consultant of the change which, of course, required different specifications and a new search.

Such changes usually occur because plans and solutions to problems have not been thought through carefully enough. In this case, the Vice President Sales had been informed of the new structure and the search, but no one had asked him what he thought about it. Too often there is a tendency to rush into an executive search when time and expense would have been saved by researching the problem more thoroughly.

6. The potential client insists on being presented with examples of candidates before authorizing a search

There are organizations that demand that the search firm must prove their ability to find the right candidate by presenting, beforehand, detailed descriptions of three or four executives already known to the firm who would fit the job specification. There are two negative aspects to this procedure.

One is that information on executives in the possession of search firms is to be treated in strictest confidence and certainly not revealed for the purpose of selling an assignment. Another negative aspect is that the ability to produce data from the files is no indicator at all of the firm's competence to conduct a thorough search, identify the best candidates, and help the client to recruit one of them into the open position.

The selection of a search firm and of the individual consultant is likely to be much more successful if their reputation and track record are carefully checked rather than judging them on the basis of people in their files.

7. Client demands immediate candidates

Very often, the decision to have a search conducted is prompted by a resignation. The incumbent is leaving in 30 days. There is no replacement. A search firm is given the assignment and is told that it is extremely urgent. Almost daily, the search consultant receives calls from his client demanding to see candidates.

A thorough search requires 45 days. If the search has to cover several countries, it may require 60 days. Attempts to pressure a search consultant to substantially reduce those periods will result in either causing him to take shortcuts or frustrating him. Bringing in an executive from outside is a vital step for any organization. It deserves the time that is required to do it thoroughly.

8. Key executives in the client organization are too busy

A major problem encountered by executive search firms is inaccessability or unavailability of the key executives involved in making decisions on candidates. The problem often begins before the search even starts, when the decision-makers cannot spare the time or are travelling or tied up in meetings and are unavailable to provide the thorough briefing necessary to enable the consultant to conduct the search effectively.

Then, when candidates are developed, no one is available to discuss them or interview them. As most candidates are not seeking a change but were persuaded by the consultant to explore the open position, they will not hang on indefinitely. They soon withdraw, either because other opportunities have developed in the meantime or with the comment that the long delay must be indicative of management's lack of interest in the open position or in their candidacy. The probability of losing a good candidate increases with every week of delay in decision making after he has expressed a willingness to be considered for the vacant position.

The current and future performance of an organization is governed by its executives. Surely their recruitment should be given top priority.

9. Failure to respect confidentiality

A search was being conducted for a Vice President Technical Services of a consumer products company. A candidate was presented who, at the time, was employed by a competitor. The Chairmen of both companies were friends and frequently played golf together. The Chairman of the company for whom the search was being conducted telephoned the Chairman of the company with which the candidate was employed and asked him for a strictly off-the-record opinion of the candidate. That same day, the candidate's compensation package was amply increased and he was given a pep talk about his future. In a different company, he could have been fired or at least classified as disloyal.

Unless a candidate is openly seeking a job, any discussions and meetings with him regarding a change of organization must be treated in strictest confidence. Otherwise, not only can the candidate be hurt, but the reputation of the hiring organization can be damaged.

10. Poor handling of candidates

The executive search consultant has clearly explained and emphasized that he had great difficulty in persuading his candidate to be interviewed. Nevertheless, the first executive in the client organization to meet the candidate immediately asks Why are you looking for a job? It would be difficult to find a quicker way of turning the candidate off, but it happens all the time.

During interviews, some client executives spend most of the time talking about themselves with almost no questions to the candidate. Key executives also tend to be poor listeners. Their opinions of the candidates are therefore superficial, but nevertheless are a deciding factor in the selection or rejection of a candidate.

When the negotiation phase is reached, there are client executives who are unprepared and inexperienced, and yet they insist on conducting the negotiations themselves. When they fail, they lose an opportunity to bring an outstanding individual into their organization.

From the first contact with a candidate, the greater the skill and consideration with which he is handled, the more likely is he to accept if offered the position or to have a positive image of the organization if he is not hired.

11. The candidate backs out at the last minute

If executive search consultants have nightmares about their work, one of them must be the loss of a candidate just before he joins the client organization. When all of the effort that is invested in a search is considered, to lose the best candidate at the eleventh hour is a disaster. Both client and consultant are usually stunned by the event and have difficulty in starting again to fill the open position.

There is much that the consultant can and should do to prevent such an occurrence, but the client organization has an equally important role during the critical period between the candidate's decision to accept the client's offer and his actually joining the client organization. When both work together and keep in close touch with the candidate, the chances of his changing his mind at the last minute are reduced.

12. Lack of consideration for the candidate after joining the client organization

The integration of the candidate into the new organization is far more complex than is generally realized. It is a process that has to be well managed. The new executive has to adapt to a different culture system. He has to establish new relationships above, below, and alongside him. He must find his way through the complicated maze of which any organization is comprised. No longer does he have a team that he has built, nor friends down the hall or upstairs with whom he can communicate easily.

Some organizations handle this problem so well that the integration is completed within a year. Others do it so badly that the process is prolonged and in some cases comes to an abrupt end after a few months. Then comes the debate. Did the executive leave because he was not the right person for the job or because he was mishandled. No matter which was the cause, the search project must be reinstated with all of the attendant direct and hidden costs, not only of two searches instead of one, but of the prolonged vacancy of a key executive position.

In summary, most of the problems encountered by executive search firms are caused either by their own deficiencies or by a lack of understanding of their role. Good executive search firms want to provide optimum service. They know that their success depends upon their reputations. Organizations that comprehend the real role of executive search firms can avoid unnecessary problems and are most likely to obtain the best results from them.

Chapter Sixteen

Guide
for Executives
Who Are Approached
as a Prospective
Candidate
by an Executive
Search Firm

When you are contacted by an executive search firm as an executive rather than as a potential client, the consultant will usually have one of three purposes in mind. Either he wants to discuss your possible candidacy for one of his assignments or he is seeking your advice on potential candidates because he respects your knowledge, contacts, and judgment or he wants to question you as a reference on a candidate whom he is considering. No matter which of these is his purpose, your first consideration should be your own reputation and image. Should this search firm and should this consultant be permitted to use your name and be entrusted with the information that you may give them? If you do not know the firm or the consultant, you would be wise to ask for and check their references before answering any of the consultant's questions.

When you are satisfied that you are dealing with a reputable firm, it is customary to cooperate with the consultant who contacts you. Most good executives who are approached as prospective candidates will at least listen to the description of the open position whether or not they are interested in a possible change. It makes sense to do so because the opportunity just might be the right one, whether or not you were thinking about making a change.

Very often, the consultant, initially, can only provide general information about his client and his assignment because of the need for strict confidentiality. He must not, usually, enable you to identify his client until he is given permission to do so by his client. This is one of the reasons why the search firm's reputation is so important to you. When the search firm is reputable, you can safely answer the consultant's questions. You are also free to refuse to go further when the client organization is finally identified to you, and you decide that you would prefer not to join it.

Normally, the consultant will describe his client and the open position in general terms and will immediately ask you whether you would be willing to explore the opportunity. At this point, and throughout your relationship with the search firm and its client, it is wise to be frank, truthful, discrete, and decisive. There are countless cases of immature executives who view the approach of an executive search consultant as an opportunity to apply leverage within their own organization. A typical example was a divisional director of quality control with a large defense contractor who, when contacted by a search consultant regarding a broader manufacturing position in another company, informed his boss, his peers, and his subordinates that he was being offered a much bigger job elsewhere. His boss viewed him as essential to the good performance of the division and reacted by raising his salary, broadening his responsibilities somewhat, and making him eligible for stock options. Having gained so many points on that occasion, this executive, during the following 15 months, tried the same ploy again. It did not work a second time. His bluff was called. Furthermore, when his boss was promoted shortly thereafter, this executive was no longer considered as a possible replacement, largely because of his behavior in trying to pressure the company into giving him more. He also lost credibility with two major executive search firms who realized that he had been trying to use them to improve his situation with his present employer.

If the opportunity described by the consultant who contacts you sounds at all interesting, all that is necessary at this stage is to express a willingness to explore it further. There is no commitment implied yet by either side. The next step will probably be an initial interview by phone for the purpose of determining whether you fit the general profile of the position. This step especially makes sense when you and the consultant are in different cities or countries, thus making a face-to-face interview expensive and time-consuming.

In conjunction with the telephone interview, the consultant will ask for your résumé. If you have one, it can save some of your and his time in providing essential information on your background. If you do not have one, there is no obligation to prepare a résumé.

The face-to-face interview with the consultant will be arranged to suit your convenience. It could well be one of the critical incidents in your career. Although you are being sought after by the consultant, you would not have agreed to an interview unless you were interested. The impression that you make will determine whether you will be recommended to the consultant's client. Certainly, it does not make sense to convey a false image, but there are some basics that should be observed. Among these are being punctual for the interview, allowing plenty of time to find and reach the meeting place. Another basic that is often overlooked is dressing appropriately and being well groomed. For example, an executive in another area of the country was being considered for a key position at the New York headquarters of a blue-chip corporation. He arrived at the consultant's hotel room dressed in a bright blue suit with trousers that were too long, tan shoes, colorful socks, and a rather flamboyant shirt and tie. The interview was a short one, and he was politely rejected.

During interviews with the consultant and subsequently with his client's executives, the basic guidelines should be frankness, truthfulness, and discretion. It is important to be a good listener. Good judgment needs to be exercised on the information that you reveal about your current employer and position. It is normal, however, to openly answer all questions regarding your current compensation package. Otherwise, neither the consultant nor his client can determine whether they can afford you.

On the matter of compensation, a mistake that is often made is to attempt to give a global figure that encompasses all of the benefits and perquisites. A typical example was an executive who, when asked to describe his compensation package, replied that it amounted to approximately $200,000. Detailed questioning finally brought out that his base salary was $110,000, his most recent bonus was $23,000, and the rest was his inflated estimate of the value of the benefits, stock options, and company car. Such responses do not make a good impression. On the other hand, during the initial discussions with the consultant on the phone, his question about your compensation can, if you prefer, be answered by saying, for example, that you would not consider a move for less than $150,000 base salary plus a substantial bonus opportunity and attractive stock options and that the salary requested could be higher if the location were more expensive than your present area of residence. This enables the consultant to decide whether his discussion with you should continue. The details of your current compensation can then be given to the consultant when he interviews you in person.

When the consultant decides that you are a probable candidate for the position, he will usually discuss references with you. He will be interested in talking with people to whom you have reported and to others who have worked closely with you. Here again, the reputation of the search firm is so important. It is unlikely that a consultant with a top firm would misuse or mishandle the references that you agree upon. You would not, of course, permit him to talk to anyone in your present company until your resignation has been accepted. He would insist that you contact the other references, who are outside your organization, to obtain their agreement—and thus their assurance of confidentiality—before they are approached by the consultant.

From the first contact with the consultant, there is the basic question as to when you should inform your present employer that you are being considered for a position with another organization. The best answer is "not until you have formally decided to accept the new job or to reject it." If you tell them beforehand, you put yourself into a no-man's land in which you are somewhere between someone who is already on his way out and an executive to be intensively courted. If you are not, in the end, offered the position, you could be looked upon by your current organization as a disloyal reject.

Many executives who are effective in managing other people are quite inept in handling themselves when considering an offer involving a change of employment. Ordinarily, they thoroughly research a proposal and consider all possible eventualities from worst case to best case. Too often, when approached as a prospective candidate for another company, they do not ask enough questions about the organization that is offering the new opportunity or about the job that is being proffered. Even more frequently, they do not think through the situations that they may face when they inform their present employer of their decision to leave. As a result, they either allow themselves to be persuaded to change their minds and stay, thus unnecessarily putting a question mark within their present organization over their judgment and reliability, or they make a change with which they are subsequently disappointed.

Supposing that, during the course of the efforts to recruit you, your boss suddenly tells you that he has become aware that you are a candidate for a position with another company. The best response is to readily admit it, giving as little information as is possible within the bounds of diplomacy and to ask the question, Wouldn't you agree to explore an attractive opportunity if you were approached by a good executive search firm?

It is wise to have a firm commitment in writing from the prospective employer prior to resigning. It should be in the form of a contractual agreement that spells out all of the important aspects of the position, all details of the compensation package, and the organization's obligations in moving you, your family, and household. In addition, of course, an adequate period of notice of termination of employment should be specified.

When you are first approached by an executive search firm as a prospective candidate, you are probably one of very many executives on their list of prospects for the position. When you are presented to the firm's client organization, you may be one of only three candidates who are under serious consideration. If you are turned down along the way, try to determine the real reason so that you can learn from the experience. If you have established a good rapport with the consultant, he may well contact you again when he is asked to undertake a similar assignment.

Chapter Seventeen

Guide
for the Executive
Who Has Decided
to Find a Position
with Another
Organization

Otherwise good executives frequently fail to effectively plan, organize, and implement a program aimed at finding a position with another organization. The entire effort needs to be viewed as a major complex project with clearly defined objectives that are thoroughly thought through and spelled out, thus greatly increasing the chances of finding the optimum job. A realistic time frame is needed to reduce the tendency toward impatience, panic, and irrational decisions. The closer to the top of the pyramid, the fewer the positions and the greater is the time needed to find the right opportunity. A year or more may be required at senior levels.

Usually, it is wiser to remain employed while you are seeking a change. In most cases, it would be inadvisable to tell your employer that you have decided to look outside. Therefore, as an employed executive, your search would have to be conducted secretly, with its attendant constraints. Under these circumstances, you have three basic ways of conducting your search. The best way is through contacts whom you can trust. Another is to increase your exposure to information on changes that are planned or that are occurring in the companies that you have targeted. The third way is through contact with executive search firms.

Search firms are a very limited means of assistance to the job seeker. They are retained and paid only by organizations to fill positions with the best executives that can be found and brought into the open position. On average, each executive search consultant is handling six assignments at any given moment. Therefore, even a large search firm has a relatively small number of opportunities on which it is working at any given moment, and the specification for each position is usually rather tight. Furthermore, a search firm that is retained by that part of your organization to which you belong cannot recruit you without formal permission from your boss.

Despite these limitations, selected search firms should be made aware, on a confidential basis, of your desire to join another organization. Listings of search firms are published by Consultants News, a publication of Kennedy and Kennedy Inc., Templeton Road, Fitzwilliam, N.H. 03447. The Association of Executive Search Consultants, 151 Railroad Avenue, Greenwich, Conn. 06830 publishes a list of its members.

The best approach to a search firm is through a good contact who is well known to one of the consultants and who thinks highly of you. In the absence of such friends, the next best approach is a brief letter with enclosed short résumé to whichever of the firm's offices is most conveniently located.

Executive job seekers sometimes find it difficult to understand that there is no point in insisting on an interview with a search firm. Such interviews waste their and your time unless they have a specific requirement for which they wish to consider you. An exception to this ground rule may occur if you are from out of town and have notified the firm in advance that you will be visiting their city. They may decide that your background is likely to be of interest for future assignments and that they should therefore take the opportunity to have a short meeting with you during your visit.

In any case, if your background is of current interest, you will immediately hear from them. If it is only of potential interest for future assignments, your information will usually be added to the firm's data system and your résumé filed for future reference. The data system would then identify you and indicate the location of your file to any of the firm's consultants who may be interested in your qualifications in the future.

Usually, the executive job seeker who carefully lists his good contacts and then systematically calls those contacts and follows up with a letter and résumé, gets the best results. A strong recommendation from an intermediary who knows you well can open many doors and bring you into contact with a variety of job opportunities. Periodic follow-up is needed to ensure that everyone is keeping you in mind.

Increasing your exposure to changes that are occurring or are planned in your target organizations largely consists of tuning your antennae and directing your attention accordingly. Normally you would only be generally or mildly interested in these events, but during the job-seeking program, keeping yourself well informed enables you to utilize your contacts more effectively by drawing their attention to the situations for which they might suggest you as a candidate.

If your employment has been terminated or if your employer has agreed that you should seek a position in another organization, you can, of course, use all possible contacts without concern over confidentiality. The question then arises as to whether you should undertake a large mailing of your résumé to dozens or even hundreds of companies. The answer depends upon the type and level of position that you are seeking. For middle management positions, a large mailing may be advisable, but at higher levels, the shotgun approach could damage your image and be counterproductive. As the most effective way of bringing you into direct positive contact with decision makers in your target companies is through executives who know you, like you, and respect you, it is inadvisable to introduce other activities into your search program that would interfere with or weaken the effectiveness of those direct contacts.

Your employer may offer to pay for the services of a professional outplacement firm if you have been discharged. Assuming that one of the good outplacement firms has been retained, they can often convert what at first seemed like a negative event in your career to a positive one. If you are not fortunate enough to have these services put at your disposal, you may explore the idea of retaining a professional firm to help you with your search. Before commiting yourself to any such firm, a very thorough check on them is essential.

Executives often put too many conditions, at the beginning of their search, on what they will or will not accept, only to have to become more flexible after they have lost some good opportunities. You may, for example, have a strong preference for a particular geographic location, but why refuse to consider anywhere else unless jobs galore are being offered to you?

Finally some advice about résumés may be helpful. The slick, printed résumé is hardly consistent with a custom-tailored job-search program. It could indicate that your résumé is probably on everyone's desk. It may also convey the idea that you are trying to impress by appearance rather than through substance. A carefully composed, cleanly typed, one- or two-page résumé presents the information that needs to be communicated in a businesslike format. Basic data such as name, birthdate, birthplace, nationality, marital status, address, phone, and education usually appear at the top. Next comes a short statement of your objectives. The clearer and more realistic they are, the more likely that they will be taken seriously. This is followed by the names of employers, position titles, and dates, in reverse chronological order. In each position, a very brief description of the function, responsibilities, and results achieved will be sufficient to give the recipient a quick understanding of your qualifications.

Index

About the Author

A. ROBERT TAYLOR is founder of TASA, one of the largest worldwide executive search firms. He has more than 30 years' experience in the human resources management field, working with major corporations in the United States and abroad.